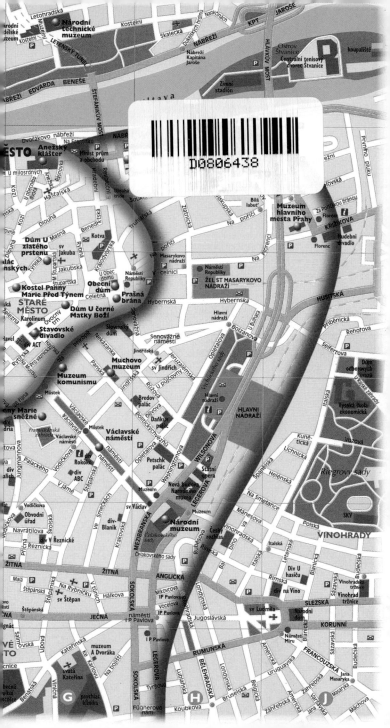

How to Use This Book

KEY TO SYMBOLS

➕ Map reference to the accompanying fold-out map

✉ Address

☎ Telephone number

🕐 Opening/closing times

🍴 Restaurant or café

🚈 Nearest rail station

Ⓜ Nearest subway (Metro) station

🚌 Nearest bus route

🚢 Nearest riverboat or ferry stop

♿ Facilities for visitors with disabilities

❓ Other practical information

▷ Further information

ℹ Tourist information

✋ Admission charges:
Expensive (more than 200Kč)
Moderate (100Kč–150Kč) and
Inexpensive (100Kč or less)

This guide is divided into four sections

• **Essential Prague:** An introduction to the city and tips on making the most of your stay.

• **Prague by Area:** We've broken the city into five areas, and recommended the best sights, shops, entertainment venues, nightlife and restaurants in each one. Suggested walks help you to explore on foot.

• **Where to Stay:** The best hotels, whether you're looking for luxury, budget or something in between.

• **Need to Know:** The info to make your trip run smoothly, including getting about by public transport, weather tips, emergency phone numbers and useful websites.

Navigation In the Prague by Area chapter, we've given each area its own color, which is also used on the locator maps throughout the book and the map on the inside front cover.

Maps The fold-out map accompanying this book is a comprehensive street plan of Prague. The grid on this fold-out map is the same as the grid on the locator maps within the book. We've given grid references within the book for each sight and listing.

Contents

Introducing Prague

Two decades after the Velvet Revolution, Prague is the short-break destination of choice for millions of visitors. Its rich culture and a miraculously preserved architectural heritage more than meet their expectations.

Built on both banks of the Vltava, and with a castle atop a rocky spur, Prague is a glorious fusion of nature and architecture. It is the very image of what a capital city was before the onset of the industrial age. Woods and orchards sweep down to the water's edge, while the skyline is pierced by myriad towers and steeples. Buildings of every era stand side by side, from burgher's house to baroque palace, from art nouveau apartment block to Cubist café. The historic hub is compact enough to be easily explored on foot (though the excellent public transport system can help take the strain).

In the 1990s, when the world started to come to a Prague that it had ignored for so long, many locals felt excluded, resentful that the city had been taken over by foreigners. Times have changed; while tourism has become a mainstay of the economy, increasingly prosperous Czechs have begun to reclaim their territory. Sleek modern hotels and daring fusion restaurants are no longer just the preserve of visitors, and bars and cafés are filled with stylish young locals.

Visitors are better catered to than ever before. As well as a growing choice of hotels and restaurants, Prague's nightlife scene is blossoming. Innovative Black Light theater delights audiences, while music lovers can choose from concerts ranging from Mozart to jazz. Once-dusty museums are modernizing, and new attractions include a museum for Franz Kafka, the city's most famous literary son. Beware of Prague's embrace! It was Kafka who warned of Prague that "this little mother has claws", and once in her grasp you may find it difficult to leave.

Facts + Figures

- Prague's population is around 1.28 million.
- Czechs drink an average of 149 liters (315 pints) of beer per person per year.
- The city has 10,000 works of art and protected objects.

THE 1,000-YEAR FLOOD

The usually tranquil Vltava can present another fiercer face, as in 1890, when its waters rose and swept away three arches of Charles Bridge. But the worst-ever flood came in August 2002, when whole districts of the city were under water, thousands of people had to be evacuated from their homes and billions of crowns of damage were caused.

PRAGUE PEOPLE

Half of Prague's 1,280,000 citizens live in *paneláks*, the high-rise, prefabricated apartment blocks of Communist times that form a ring around the city. Originally of low-quality construction, many *paneláks* have been modernized and upgraded. Some of the housing complexes now include schools, libraries, shopping complexes and even swimming pools.

VISITORS TO THE RESCUE

Even before Communism, Prague was an important manufacturing base, and the totalitarian regime promoted industries of all kinds. In recent years tourism has taken over from industry as the city's big earner, helping to keep levels of unemployment at virtually zero and income much higher than in the rest of the country.

A Short Stay in Prague

DAY 1

Morning Start on the steps in front of the **Národní Muzeum** (▷ 48) with a view down Václavské náměstí. Go through the underpass to the statue of Good King Wenceslas, then walk down the square. Look into the Lucerna Passage and admire mischievous artist David Černý's zany take on the Wenceslas statue. At the foot of the square, head west along 28 října and Národní třída to catch the No. 22 (Bílá Hora) tram from the stop behind the My store. Enjoy the ride across the **River Vltava** (▷ 52), through Malá Strana and up to Pražský hrad. Linger in the courtyards, looking into the Old Royal Palace, **Katedrála sv Víta** (▷ 68) and Golden Lane. Descend to Malá Strana via steep **Nerudova** (▷ 89), marvel at the baroque interior of **Chrám sv Mikuláše** (▷ 84), then go through the lanes to tranquil Kampa Island.

Lunch Enjoy lunch in the riverside restaurant attached to the **Museum Kampa** (▷ 89).

Afternoon Cross the Vltava via **Karlův most** (▷ 28) and lose yourself among the labyrinthine lanes of the Old Town before finding your way to **Staroměstské náměstí** (▷ 32), making sure that you are there on the hour to see the Astronomical Clock in action.

Dinner Tuck into a substantial Czech feast of duck, cabbage and dumplings at one of the Kolkovna group's superpubs, for example **Kolkovna** (▷ 41).

Evening Continue your night out in one of the city's traditional pubs such as **U Fleků** (▷ 62) or **U Medvídků** (▷ 42).

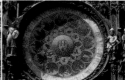

DAY 2

Morning Board tram 22 at a convenient point and ride to the Pohořelec stop. Admire the halls of **Strahovský klášter** (▷ 74) then soak up the glorious city panorama. Catch the carillon at the **Loreta** (▷ 70) and time your arrival at the western entrance of the castle to watch the midday changing of the guard. Go down to Malá Strana via Nové zámecké schody (New Castle Steps) and walk through **Valdštejnský palác** (▷ 88) and its garden to the little riverside park at the end of Mánes Bridge. Here you can pause for a break and take in the unusual view across the river to Charles Bridge and the Old Town.

Lunch Enjoy a meal at the **Hergetova cihelna** restaurant (▷ 94).

Afternoon Retrace your steps to Malostranská station and travel two stops to Můstek. On emerging from the station, walk northeastwards along Na Příkopě, one of the city's foremost shopping streets, to the **Prašná brána (Powder Tower,** ▷ 36) and the **Obecní dům (Municipal House,** ▷ 30). After a conducted tour of the fabulous art nouveau interiors of the Municipal House, relax with coffee and cakes in its sumptuous café. Afterward, go a short distance along Celetná, admiring the Black Madonna building before turning right through a passageway to Štupártská and Malá Štupartská, then beneath the archway into Týn Court. Cross Old Town Square to the Pařížská shopping boulevard and **Josefov** (▷ 26), visiting the Old/New Synagogue and the Old Jewish Cemetery.

Dinner Dine at a restaurant with a view—**Petřínské terasy** (▷ 94).

Evening Be thrilled by opera or ballet in the **Národní divadlo** (▷ 60).

ESSENTIAL PRAGUE **TOP 25**

This is a quick guide to the Top 25, which are described in more detail later. Here they are listed alphabetically, and the tinted background shows the area they are in.

HRADČANY
63-80

STARÉ MĚSTO
20-42

MALÁ STRANA
81-94

NOVÉ MĚSTO
43-62

Shopping

It's increasingly hard for visitors to escape uniformity and find local products worth taking home. Thanks to their long tradition as craftspeople and artisans, however, the Czechs have plenty to offer. Along with crystal and garnets, don't overlook the herbal liqueur Becherovka, blue onion porcelain and art books. Christmas markets are gloriously festive, filling the main squares throughout December, while giant modern malls offer all-weather convenience.

Antiques

Antiques stores, found under signs reading *starožítnictví, bazar* or *vetešnictví* (junk shop), contain many treasures to take home: Quality paintings, kitchenware, jewelry and linens can be found at reasonable prices. Many bazaars specialize in old cameras, clocks and other mechanical devices.

Fashion

A number of Czech fashion designers are making a name for themselves and have opened successful boutiques where you can find original pieces at a fraction of what you would pay at home for an item of similar quality. Most of these shops are concentrated on a few streets north of Old Town Square—Dlouhá, Dušní and V Kolkovně. Fashionable international names line nearby Pařížska, but don't expect bargains there.

SPA TREATS

A whole culture has grown up around Czech spa towns. Re-create this atmosphere at home by strolling about, drinking water from a porcelain cup with a built-in straw and sipping spa waters, or *oplátky*. The cups can be found cheaply in many of the city's antiques shops. Round off your cure with a shot of Becherovka, the herbal liqueur developed by a spa doctor in Karlovy Vary in 1807. It's said to be especially good for anyone suffering from a stomach ailment.

From antique books to toys and painted eggs to glass, Prague has plenty of good souvenir choices

Books

Considering the Czechs' contribution to art, architecture and photography, it's not surprising that handsome coffee-table books devoted to subjects such as Czech cubism, avant-garde photography and the art nouveau movement are popular.

Glassware

Glass and crystal, of course, are ubiquitous, and the sheer number of shops and variety of products can be overwhelming. But Czech crystal is famous for a reason and should not be overlooked. Stick to shops affiliated with just one or two manufacturers that focus primarily on tableware and larger individual pieces and you're likely to take home something of real quality. Look for hand-blown, hand-cut lead crystal produced by names such as Moser and Sklo Bohemia, and Desná for art deco styles.

Souvenirs

Much of what is sold in the tourist areas bears no relation to local traditions or culture: Russian dolls and mass-produced lace tablecloths, Polish amber and non-Czech crystal. If one of these products catches your eye and doesn't break the bank there's nothing wrong in buying it—but if your heart is set on a real Czech souvenir, keep looking.

NOT ALL GARNETS ARE CREATED EQUAL

The Czechs have been mining garnets for centuries. Said to bring vitality and cure depression, the Bohemian variety of garnet is not found anywhere else in the world. They are a deep, rich red known as "dove's blood" and the settings typically feature many small garnets clustered together. Most garnet jewelry is made by the cooperative Granát Turnov and sold in factory stores and by authorized dealers with a stamp of approval. However, a fair amount of what is sold in Prague as Bohemian garnets is actually made from almandines or other stones from Italy and elsewhere. Showy gold pieces set with large, brownish stones are not Bohemian garnets.

Shopping by Theme

Whether you're looking for a department store, a quirky boutique, or something in between, you'll find it all in Prague. On this page shops are listed by theme. For a more detailed write-up, see the individual listings in Prague by Area.

ANTIQUES

Ahasver Antiques (▷ 92)
Alma Antique (▷ 38)
Dorotheum (▷ 38)
Hodinářství Matouš (▷ 57)
Modernista (▷ 39)

ARTS AND CRAFTS

Galerie Peithner-Lichtenfels (▷ 38)
Shevchuk Art Gallery (▷ 79)

BOOKS

Academia (▷ 57)
Antikvariát Gallerie Můstek (▷ 57)
Antikvariát Karel Křenek (▷ 38)
Antikvariát Pařížská (▷ 38)
Globe Bookstore and Coffeehouse (▷ 57)
Kiwi (▷ 58)
Knihkupectvi Tynska (▷ 39)
Palác Knih Luxor (▷ 58)
Prazsky Almanach (▷ 92)

COSMETICS

Botanicus (▷ 38)

FASHION

Boheme (▷ 38)
Elazar (▷ 57)
Kožešiny Kubín (▷ 92)
Myslivost (▷ 58)
Timoure et Group (▷ 39)

FOOD AND WINE

Bistro Deli and Bakery (▷ 57)
Cellarius (▷ 57)
Country Life (▷ 38)
Culinaria (▷ 38)
Havelský trh (▷ 39)
Víno Ungelt (▷ 39)
Zlatý Kříz (▷ 58)

GLASS AND CERAMICS

Art Deco (▷ 38)
Artěl (▷ 38)
Celetná Crystal (▷ 38)
Dům Porcelánu (▷ 57)
Moser (▷ 58)

HANDICRAFTS AND SOUVENIRS

Manufaktura (▷ 39)
Museum Shop (▷ 79)
Qubus (▷ 39)

JEWELRY

Granát (▷ 39)
Mineralia (▷ 58)

MUSIC

Agharta (▷ 38)
Bontonland (▷ 57)
Kliment (▷ 58)
Široký dvůr (▷ 79)
Via Musica (▷ 92)

PHOTOGRAPHY

Centrum Fotoškoda (▷ 57)

STORES

Baťa (▷ 57)
Lucerna Passage (▷ 58)
My (▷ 58)
Palladium (▷ 39)
Slovanský dům (▷ 58)

TOYS AND GAMES

Hracký (▷ 79)
Loutky Marionety (▷ 92)
Truhlar Marionety (▷ 39)

Prague by Night

Prague has no shortage of hip dance clubs and trendy bars, but for most Czechs the best nights are spent in a pub. No visitor to the city should pass up the opportunity to taste an expertly poured Pilsner or Budvar at the long wooden tables of a typical Czech pub. An alternative is the *vinárna* (wine bar). A *vinárna* can be a restaurant, but more typically is a small establishment—sometimes with standing room only—offering inexpensive Czech wines, often of surprisingly good quality.

All That Jazz
Czechs are known for being a musical nation and on any given night there are a variety of concerts on offer, from local modern jazz fixtures like Emil Viklický, to touring Balkan gypsy bands and performances of Dvořák and Smetana. Postage-stamp sized jazz joints abound in downtown, while larger venues like Roxy (▷ 40) and Palác Akropolis (▷ 60) book an eclectic mix of acts.

Staying Out Late
Night owls thirsty for a cocktail should head for the bars just north of Old Town Square. Another district that's home to hip bars and clubs is along Karoliny světlé near the embankment south of Old Town. Of course you can always take a romantic stroll and view the floodlit castle from the blissfully empty Charles Bridge.

There are a variety of night-time activities: traditional dancing, classical music, clubs and pubs

---

WHAT'S ON

● The best source of information for English-language readers about what's on in Prague is probably the tabloid "Night and Day" section of the weekly newspaper *Prague Post*.
● Tickets for events can be obtained at box offices (which may be less expensive) or through Ticketpro (☎ www.ticketpro.cz) or Bohemia Ticket (☎ 224 227 832; www.bohemiaticket.cz), both of which have desks at tourist information centers and some hotels.

Eating Out

Traditional Czech food is similar to other central European regional cuisines. Most dishes are built around pork, with the national dish being roast pork, served with thinly sliced bread dumplings and a sweetish sauerkraut—known to locals as *vepřo/ knedlo/zelo*.

More Preferences
Particularly popular is goulash—*guláš*. Another dish to look for is *svíčková*—a strip of beef tenderloin, served in gravy and topped with cranberry relish and a lemon. You'll also usually find very good roast duck or veal. Desserts are a high point, in particular fruit dumplings, filled with strawberries or apricots and topped with icing. The best place to find Czech food is at a traditional pub, where you can wash it down with a glass of some of the world's best beer.

International and Fast-Food Dining
Prague is filled with restaurants from all around the world and the quality is rising every year. Unfortunately, Prague is no longer considered a cheap place to eat. As for fast food, McDonald's, KFC and Starbucks are all here, along with the local competitors.

Drinks
Czechs are world famous for the quality of their beer. Light lagers are still far and away the most common, but increasingly brewers are adding dark beers to their lineups. The most popular spirits include the ever-present *slivovice*, a high-octane plum brandy.

WHERE TO DINE

With a wide choice of places to eat in the city, it's worthwhile choosing somewhere with a distinctive setting, of which there are many. You can dine in the stately ambience of an historic palace, sit at a table with a stunning view over spires and rooftops or the swiftly flowing Vltava, or enjoy a hearty repast beneath the vaults of a medieval cellar.

From grand old eateries to modern-day sandwich outlets you will find a good range of cuisine

Restaurants by Cuisine

There are restaurants to suit all tastes and budgets in Prague. On this page they are listed by cuisine. For a more detailed description of each restaurant, see Prague by Area.

AMERICAN

Bakeshop (▷ 41)
Bohemia Bagel (▷ 93)

ASIAN

Yami (▷ 42)

CAFÉS

Bar Bar (▷ 93)
Café Louvre (▷ 61)
Café Savoy (▷ 93)
Globe Bookstore and
    Coffeehouse (▷ 57)
Imperial (▷ 61)
Kavárna Evropa (▷ 61)
Lobkowicz Palace (▷ 80)
Slavia (▷ 42)
Terasa zlaté studně
    (▷ 80)
Velryba (▷ 62)
Zlatý Kříž (▷ 58)

CZECH

Ferdinanda (▷ 61)
Hybernia (▷ 61)
Kolkovna (▷ 41)
Kolkovna Olympia
    (▷ 94)
Lokal (▷ 41)
Lví dvůr (▷ 80)
Novoměstský pivovar
    (▷ 61)
Petřínské terasy (▷ 94)
Plzeňská restaurace
    (▷ 41)
Pod křídlem (▷ 62)

Potrefena Husá (▷ 42)
Sovovy mlýny (▷ 94)
Terasa u zlaté hrušky
    (▷ 80)
U Císařů (▷ 80)
U Kalicha (▷ 62)
U Medvídků (▷ 42)
U modré Kachničky
    (▷ 94)
U modré Kachničky II
    (▷ 42)
U Pinkasů (▷ 62)
U Šuterů (▷ 62)

FISH

Alcron (▷ 61)
Sage (▷ 42)

FRENCH

Café de Paris (▷ 93)
Chez Marcel (▷ 41)
Le Terroir (▷ 42)
U bile kravy (▷ 62)

INTERNATIONAL

Aquarius (▷ 93)
Bellevue (▷ 41)
Coda (▷ 93)
Gitanes (▷ 93)
Hergetova Cihelna
    (▷ 94)
Hotel Questenberk
    (▷ 80)
Kampa Park (▷ 94)
Nebozízek (▷ 94)
Pálffy palác (▷ 94)
Pizzeria Kmotra (▷ 62)

Tri Stoleti (▷ 94)
Triton (▷ 62)
Universal (▷ 62)
Villa Richter (▷ 80)
V Zátíší (▷ 42)
Zlatá Praha (▷ 42)

ITALIAN

Amici Miei (▷ 41)
CottoCrudo (▷ 41)
Pizza Nuova (▷ 41)

KOSHER

King Solomon (▷ 41)

PUBS

Baracnicka Rychta
    (▷ 93)
Černý Orel (▷ 93)
Hoffa (▷ 61)
Pivovarský Dům (▷ 62)
U Fleků (▷ 62)
U Vejvodů (▷ 42)

SPANISH

El Centro (▷ 93)

VEGETARIAN

Govinda Vegetarian
    Restaurant and Club
    (▷ 61)
Maitrea (▷ 41)

Top Tips For...

However you'd like to spend your time in Prague, these top suggestions should help you tailor your ideal visit. Each suggestion has a fuller write-up elsewhere in the book.

UNUSUAL ANTIQUES

Enhance your appreciation of Bohemian glass and porcelain by studying the stunning exhibits at the Uměleckoprůmyslové muzeum (UPM—Decorative Arts Museum, ▷ 34).

Avoid the souvenir shops along the tourist trail, and look instead at the Dorotheum (▷ 38).

Search for a bargain at one of the reputable antiques establishments such as Alma Antique (▷ 38).

HISTORIC HOTELS

Look for luxurious lodgings behind the baroque facade of the Hotel Aria (▷ 112) in Malá Strana.

Take up residence in the Mandarin Oriental Hotel (▷ 112), an exquisitely sensitive conversion of a 14th-century monastery in the quietest part of Malá Strana.

Luxuriate in the stylish K&K Central Hotel (▷ 112), a jewel of art nouveau architecture and interior design.

Glassware and antiques are worth seeking out in Prague

DINING WITH A VIEW

Dine with a table-side view of Prague Castle at Bellevue (▷ 41).

Stroll down from the castle and relax on the terraces of the elegant Villa Richter (▷ 80).

Enjoy countrified views from Petřínské terasy, perched amid the greenery of Petřín Hill (▷ 94).

Gaze down over Malá Strana from Terasa u zlaté studně (▷ 80), tucked away against the Castle ramparts.

Many Prague hotels are in grand old buildings (above right); the restaurant at the top of the Dancing House building has great views (right)

Try local fare to get a true taste of the city

CZECH COOKING

Tuck into traditional Czech food prepared as if it were haute cuisine at U modré Kachničky I or II (▷ 42, 94).

Sate your appetite with hearty Bohemian fare at U Pinkasů (▷ 62), and wash it down with well-kept Pilsner Urquell.

Enjoy duck and dumplings at Kolkovna (▷ 41), a refined version of the classic Czech pub.

BEING PAMPERED

Learn how to relax totally in the wellness area of one of the city's luxury hotels (some of which are open to non-guests). The superb spa that is part of the Mandarin Oriental Hotel (▷ 112) is in a league of its own.

Find your way to the Sabai Studio in the Slovanský dům arcade (▷ 58), and submit to the attentions of qualified massage therapists, whose treatments have been developed in Thailand for more than a thousand years.

Find your own way to relax—at a spa or enjoying a massage

GREAT JAZZ

Force your way into the cramped basement of U malěho Glena (▷ 92) to soak up some of the city's best jazz.

Descend into a Gothic cellar at Agharta Jazz Centrum (▷ 40) for an evening you won't forget, with some of the top names in jazz performing regularly.

Ignore the misleading name (The Old Lady), hot sessions are a nightly rule at Jazz Lounge U staré paní (▷ 40).

Live music—be it jazz, traditional or contemporary—can be enjoyed in a variety of venues

KEEPING THE KIDS HAPPY

There are activities to involve your children

Take them to the Mirror Maze (Bludiště, ▷ 87) at the top of Petřín Hill and watch them split their sides at the distorting mirrors.

Visit the amusement park at Výstaviště Praha (▷ 104), or the nearby Planetarium. Then continue out of town to the Zoo.

Keep small children amused on a rainy day by taking them to see the rainbow-colored tropical fish at Mořský svět (▷ 103), within the Výstaviště Praha. The aquarium's feeding tanks are particularly popular.

GETTING UP HIGH

Escape the crowds and climb the Old Town Bridge Tower (▷ 28) for a bird's-eye view of Charles Bridge.

Toil up the endless steps of the tower of Chrám sv Mikuláše (▷ 84) and emerge high above the red rooftops of Malá Strana.

Climb toward heaven via the winding staircase of the south tower of Katedrála sv Víta (▷ 68) for a panorama that is otherwise enjoyed only by angels.

SEEING THE CITY IN STYLE

Take to the water for a pleasure cruise along the Vltava (▷ 52).

Hop aboard a vintage tram (▷ 119) for a nostalgic trip along the tracks.

Take the little funicular to the top of Petřín Hill for a spectacular panorama over the city (▷ 87, 118).

Take to the waters to see the city from the Vltava River. Boat trips head downstream and most pass under five bridges (right); view from Chrám sv Mikulas over Malá Strana (above right)

Prague by Area

STARÉ MĚSTO

HRADČANY

MALÁ STRANA

FARTHER AFIELD

Staré Město

Within the Old Town's labyrinth of lanes is the greatest concentration of Prague's historic buildings, plus intriguing shops, bars and restaurants. Close by is Josefov, the historic Jewish quarter.

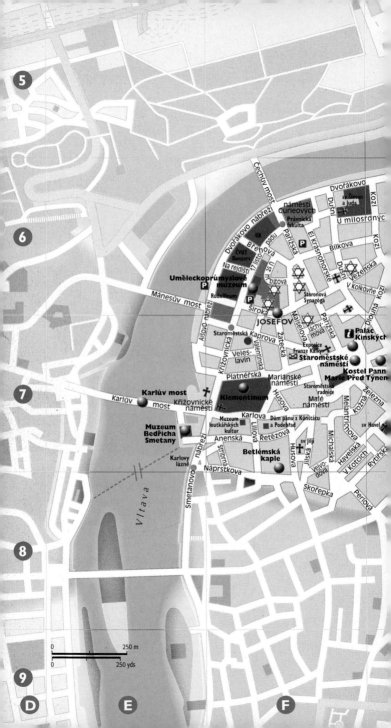

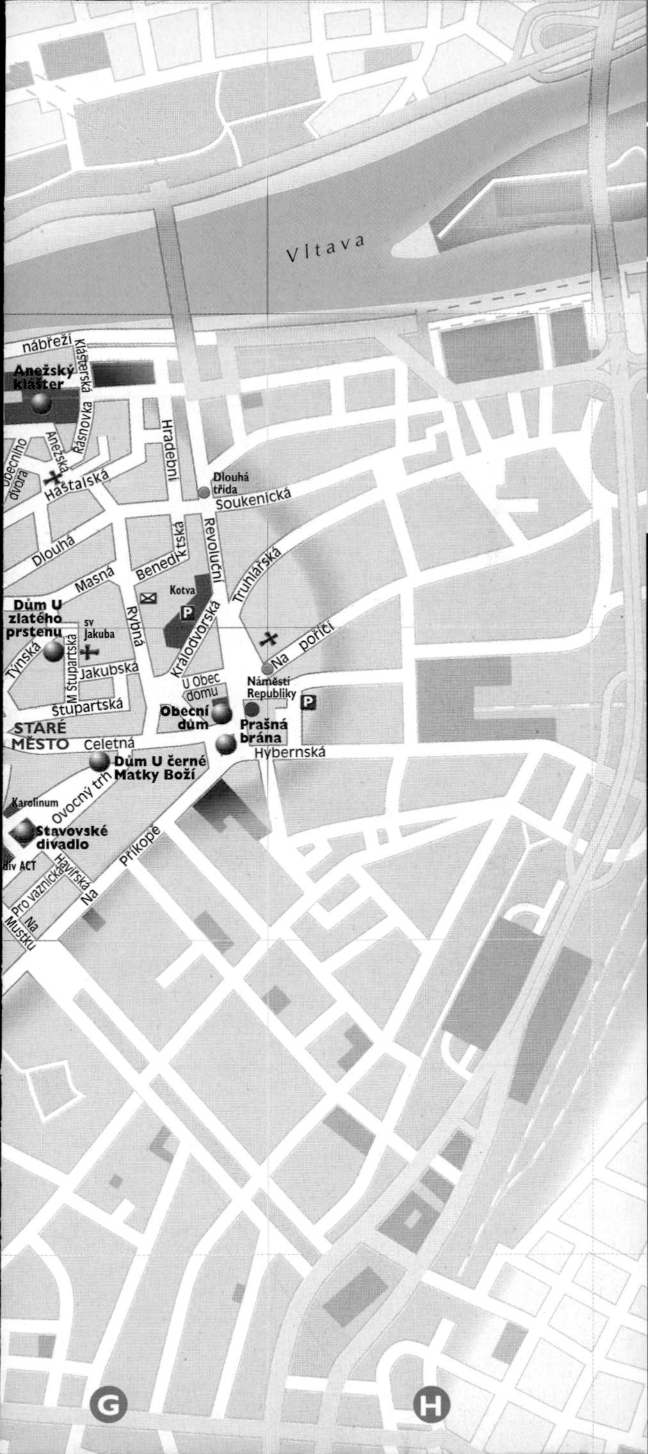

V l t a v a

nábřeží

Anežský
klášter

Obecního
dvora

Anežská

Pásnovska

Klášterská

Haštalská

Hradební

Dlouhá
třída

Soukenická

Dlouhá

Masná

Benediktská

Revoluční

Truhlářská

Na poříčí

Dům U
zlatého
prstenu

sv
Jakuba

Rybná

Kotva

Králodvorská

Týnská

U M Štupartská

Jakubská

Štupartská

U Obec
domu

Náměstí
Republiky

STARÉ
MĚSTO

Celetná

Obecní
dům

Prašná
brána

Hybernská

Dům U černé
Matky Boží

Karolinum

Ovocný trh

Stavovské
divadlo

div ACT

Havířská

Na Příkopě

Na
Můstku

Pro vaznické

G   H

Anežský klášter

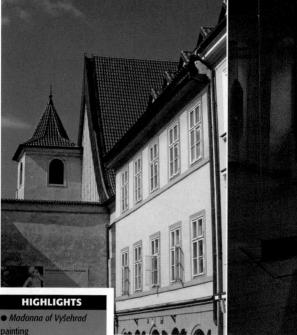

HIGHLIGHTS

- *Madonna of Vyšehrad* painting
- *Madonna and Child* sculpture from Český Krumlov
- Panel paintings by the Master of Vyšší Brod
- Portraits of saints by Master Theodoricus
- *Christ on the Mount of Olives* by the Třeboň Master
- Votive altarpiece from Zlíchov
- *Madonna of Poleň*, Cranach the Elder
- Vaulted medieval cloister
- Church of St. Francis (concert hall)
- Church of the Holy Savior

St. Agnes's Convent, the city's most venerable Gothic complex, shelters in a quiet precinct of the Old Town. Once earmarked for destruction, it is now the fitting home for one of the country's most distinctive galleries.

Canonized Czech Agnes was a 13th-century princess and founder of a convent of Poor Clares here. In its glory days St. Agnes's was a mausoleum for the royal family, but it was sacked by the Hussites in the 15th century. In 1782, it was closed down by Joseph II, and became slum housing until city authorities decided to raze it in the 1890s, only relenting when faced with bitter public protest. The convent was slowly restored, and, in November 1989, days before the Communist regime

Church of Sv František (St. Francis of Assisi) in Anežský klášter (left); the altarpiece called Resurrection by the Master of the Trebon, 1380, in Anežský klášter (middle); Church of Sv Salvator, Holy Savior (right)

ended, Agnes was made a saint. An auspicious omen, perhaps?

Medieval masterpieces The convent now displays the National Gallery's collection of medieval art from Czech lands and nearby. The magnificent works show the achievements in the fine arts in Bohemia, and above all during the reigns of Emperor Charles IV and his successors. Prague's court artists fused Italian, French and Flemish influences in a manner all their own, pointing toward the late-Gothic style that flourished in Europe.

Look down The vista to St. Agnes's Convent from Letná Plain on the far side of the Vltava gives a fascinating overview of this medieval riverside complex of buildings.

THE BASICS

www.ngprague.cz

✚ G6

✉ U Milosrdných 17

☎ 224 810 628

🕐 Tue–Sun 10–6

🚇 Náměstí Republiky

🚊 Tram 17, 18 (Právnická fakulta stop) or tram 5, 8, 14 (Dlouhá třída stop)

♿ Fair

💵 Moderate

Josefov

- Vine carving in entrance portal
- Tombstone of Rabbi Loew (1525–1609) in the Old Jewish Cemetery

TIP

- Remember that the Old/New Synagogue is still a place of worship for the Jewish community, and that men should cover their heads, both here and in the cemetery (paper *kippah* are available).

With its synagogues and age-old cemetery, Josefov is one of the most evocative sites of Jewish heritage anywhere, testimony to a world that lasted for a thousand years until brought to an end by the brutal Nazi occupation.

Ghetto memories Josefov owes its name to the liberal Emperor Josef II, who emancipated the Jews in 1781, but the ghetto itself dates from the 13th century, when its high walls kept its inhabitants in and the Christian residents out. Over time it produced many remarkable characters, foremost among them learned Rabbi Loew, creator of that archetypal man-made monster, the Golem. The ghetto's warren of twisting lanes and dark courtyards was swept away in an effort to clean up the city in the late

Clockwise from far left: Maiselova Synagoga; Španělská Synagoga or Spanish Synagogue; view along Kaprova Street; art nouveau detail on Kaprova street; statue of a walking headless figure with Franz Kafka; art nouveau apartments; the emblem of the Prague Jewish Community (replica) in the Maiselova Synagoga

19th century, when only its synagogues, cemetery and rococo Town Hall were spared. During World War II, the Nazis deported nearly all of Prague's Jews to the prison town of Terezín and then to Auschwitz. Some of the valuables they stole from Jewish communities are now on display in the synagogues.

The Old/New Synagogue With its pointed brick gable and atmospheric interior, the Gothic synagogue of 1275 is the oldest functioning in Europe, a compelling reminder of the age-old intertwining of Jewish and Christian cultures.

Old Jewish Cemetery The total number laid to rest beneath the dappled shade of the tall trees may amount to 100,000, laid on top of one another, up to 12 deep in places.

THE BASICS

✚ F6/7
✉ Cemetery: enter through Pinkas Synagogue Široka 3
☎ Jewish Museum: 222 749 211; www.jewishmuseum.cz
🕐 Jewish Museum: 31 Mar–23 Oct Sun–Fri 9–6; 25 Oct–29 Mar 9–4.30. Closed Saturdays and Jewish holidays. Old/New Synagogue: Sun–Fri 11–5. Closed Saturdays and Jewish holidays
🚇 Staroměstska
♿ Fair
💰 Cemetery/museums: expensive. Old/New Synagogue: expensive

Karlův most

HIGHLIGHTS

● Old Town Bridge Tower
● Malá Strana Bridge Tower
(viewpoint)
● Nepomuk statue with
bronze relief panels
● Bruncvík (Roland column)
to southwest
● Statue of St. John of Matha
● Bronze crucifix with
Hebrew inscription
● Statue of St. Luthgard
(by Braun)

TIP

● To experience a non-
crowded Charles Bridge you
need to get there early in the
morning, even out of season.

Any time is right to visit Charles Bridge, the medieval crossing over the Vltava. Barter with its street traders, then enjoy the almost sinister dusk, when sculpted saints on the parapets gesticulate against the darkening sky.

Gothic overpass For centuries Karlův most was Prague's only bridge, built on the orders of Emperor Charles IV in the 14th century. It's a triumph of Gothic engineering, with 16 massive sandstone arches carrying it more than 516m (564 yards) from the Old Town to soar across the Vltava River and Kampa Island to touch down near the heart of Malá Strana. It is pro-tected by sturdy timber cutwaters and guarded at both ends by towers; the eastern face of the Old Town Bridge Tower is richly ornamented. Its

Clockwise from far left: People passing artists and vendors on Charles Bridge; statue of St. John Nepomuk; tourist boat passing under Charles Bridge; the clock of the Old Town water tower; statues and buskers line the bridge; looking down alongside the bridge toward Malá Strana

opposite number has a smaller tower, once part of the earlier Judith Bridge.

Starry saint Charles Bridge has always been much more than a river crossing. Today's traders succeed earlier merchants and stallholders, and tournaments, battles and executions have all been held on the bridge. The heads of the Protestants executed in 1621 in Old Town Square were displayed here. Later that century the bridge was beautified with baroque sculptures, including the statue of St. John Nepomuk. Falling foul of the king, this unfortunate cleric was pushed off the bridge in a sack. As his body bobbed in the water, five stars are said to have danced on the surface. Nepomuk hence became the patron saint of bridges, and is always depicted with his starry halo.

THE BASICS

- ✚ E7
- ✉ Staroměstská
- Ⓜ Staroměstská
- 🚌 Tram 12, 20, 22, 23 to Malostranské náměstí
- ♿ Good
- ✋ Bridge free

Obecní dům

Exterior and interior views of the Municipal House

THE BASICS

www.obecnidum.cz

⊞ G7

✉ Náměstí Republiky 5

☎ 222 002 121; ticket office (tours and concerts): 222 002 101, daily 10–8

🕐 Check locally for times of daily guided tours

🚇 Náměstí Republiky

♿ Few

✋ Guided tour of interiors expensive

HIGHLIGHTS

● Entrance canopy and mosaic *Homage to Prague*

● Smetanova síň (Smetana Hall), with frescoes symbolizing the dramatic arts

● Mayor's Suite, with paintings by Mucha

● Riegr Hall, with Myslbek sculptures

● Palacký Room, with paintings by Preisler

The prosaic name Municipal House fails utterly to convey anything of the character of this extraordinary art nouveau building, a gloriously extravagant early-20th-century confection on which every artist of the day seems to have left his stamp.

City council citadel Glittering like a gigantic, flamboyant jewel, the Obecní dům is linked to the blackened Prašná brána (Powder Tower, ▷ 36), last relic of the Old Town's fortifications and long one of the city's main symbols. The intention of the city fathers in the first years of the 20th century was to add an even more powerful element to the cityscape that would celebrate the glory of the Czech nation and Prague's place within it. The site of the old Royal Palace was selected, and no expense spared to erect a structure in which the city's burgeoning life could expand. Begun in 1902, the great edifice was opened in 1911.

Ornamental orgy The building schedule included meeting and assembly rooms, cafés, restaurants, bars, even a pâtisserie, while the mayor was provided with particularly luxurious quarters. The 1,200-seat Smetana Hall, home of the Prague Symphony Orchestra, is a temple to the muse of Bohemian music. Everything is encrusted with lavish decoration—in stucco, glass, mosaic, murals, metalwork and textiles— not least the famous café, the gourmet French restaurant and the basement beer hall.

Staroměstské náměstí

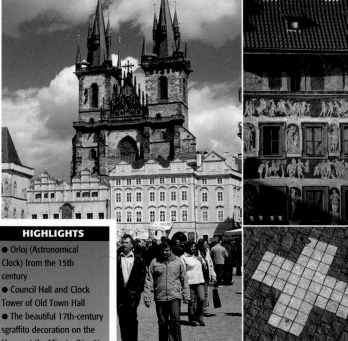

HIGHLIGHTS

● Orloj (Astronomical Clock) from the 15th century
● Council Hall and Clock Tower of Old Town Hall
● The beautiful 17th-century sgraffito decoration on the House at the Minute (No. 2)
● Kostel sv Mikuláše (the baroque Church of St. Nicholas)
● Jan Hus Memorial of 1915
● Palác Kinských (▷ 36)
● The Gothic Dům u Kamenného Zvonu (House at the Stone Bell)
● Arcaded houses Nos. 22–26, with baroque facades and medieval interiors

TIP

● Climb the tower of the Old Town Hall for one of the best views over Prague's red-tiled roofs.

Visitors throng the Old Town Square all year, entertained by street performers, refreshed at outdoor cafés and enchanted by the Astronomical Clock and the cheerful facades of the old buildings.

Martyrs and mournful memories The Old Town Square has not always been so jolly. The marketplace became a scene of execution of Hussites in the 15th century and 27 prominent Protestants were put to death in 1621 (they are commemorated by white crosses in the paving stones). In 1945, in a final act of spite, diehard Nazis demolished a whole wing of the Old Town Hall; the site has still not been built on.

Striking clock First installed during the 15th century, the Orloj (Astronomical Clock) shows

Clockwise from far left: Old Town Square with Týn Church in the background; sgraffito decoration on the House at the Minute; the square in the sunshine; the painted calendar below the Astronomical Clock; one of the 27 white crosses, which are set in the paving stones before the chapel

the position of the sun, moon and stars, while its lower dial shows the signs of the Zodiac and the changes of the seasons. Its hourly procession of carved figures is one of the city's great spectacles.

Around the square The hub of the square is the Jan Hus Memorial, an amazing art nouveau sculpture whose base is one of the few places in the square where you can sit without having to buy a drink. To one side rise the blackened towers of the Týn Church (▷ 36), while to the other is the Old Town Hall, an attractively varied assembly of buildings and, a bit farther, the city's second St. Nicholas's Church. The fine town houses surrounding the square are a study in various architectural styles from Gothic to baroque, rococo, and finally Gothic Revival.

THE BASICS

🔲 F7
✉ Staroměstské náměstí
🕐 Clock Tower: Apr–Sep daily 10–10; Oct, Mar 10–8; Nov–Feb 10–6. Town Hall: Tue–Sun 9–6, Mon 11–6
🍴 Restaurants and cafés
Ⓜ Staroměstská
♿ Fair

Uměleckoprůmyslové muzeum

Stained glass (left); the exterior of the museum (middle); an exhibit (right)

THE BASICS

www.upm.cz
F6
17 listopadu 2
251 093 111
Tue 10–7, Wed–Sun 10–6
Café (Mon–Fri 10–7, Sat, Sun 10.30–6)
Staroměstská
Tram 17, 18
Some
Moderate

HIGHLIGHTS

● *Pietra dura* scene of a town by Castnicci
● Boulle commode and cabinet
● Monumental baroque furniture by Dientzenhofer and Santini
● Meissen Turk on a rhino
● Holic porcelain figures
● Harrachov glass
● Klášterec figurines of Prague characters
● Biedermeier cradle
● Surprise view down into the Old Jewish Cemetery

The pompous facade of Prague's Decorative Arts Museum merely hints at the riches within. A steep flight of stairs leads visitors to treasure chambers full of fine furniture, glass, porcelain, clocks and more.

Riverside reclaimed Looking something like a miniature Louvre, the Decorative Arts Museum was built in 1901 in an area that, by the end of the 19th century, had turned its back on the river and become a jumble of storage depots and timber yards. The city leaders decided to beautify it with fine public buildings and riverside promenades. The School of Arts and Crafts (1884) and the Rudolfinum concert hall and gallery (1890) preceded the museum; the University's Philosophy Building (1929), which completed the enclosure of what is now Jan Palach Square, followed it.

Decorative delights The museum's collections are incredibly diverse, numbering nearly 200,000 objects from all over the world, but with special emphasis on the glorious craft heritage of the Czech lands. Carefully chosen items are arranged in a series of imaginative themed displays such as "Story of the Fiber"(covering textiles of all kinds), "Born in Fire" (glass and porcelain) and "Print and Image" (books, graphics and photography). While there are objects from every era, the contribution on the art nouveau and art deco movements are particularly rich.

More to See

BETLÉMSKÁ KAPLE (BETHLEHEM CHAPEL)

You must see this barnlike structure where Jan Hus preached to really appreciate the deeply nonconformist traditions so thoroughly obscured by centuries of imposed Catholicism. The chapel, in the Old Town, was totally reconstructed in the 1950s.

➕ F7 ✉ Betlémské náměstí 🕐 Apr–Oct Mon–Sun 10–6.30; Nov–Mar 10–5.30 🍴 Restaurants and cafés nearby 🚇 Národní třída ✋ Inexpensive

DŮM U ČERNÉ MATKY BOŽÍ (HOUSE OF THE BLACK MADONNA)

This striking example of Czech cubist architecture, designed by Josef Gočár (1912), stands squarely at the corner of Celetná Street in the heart of the Old Town. It houses a fine collection of Czech Cubism.

➕ G7 ✉ Ovocný trh 19 ☎ 224 211 746 🕐 Tue–Sun 10–6 🚇 Náměstí Republiky ✋ Moderate

DŮM U ZLATÉHO PRSTENU (HOUSE AT THE GOLDEN RING)

The Prague City Gallery's fine collection of 20th- and 21st-century Czech art is housed here. The gallery stages large exhibitions a few steps away at the House at the Stone Bell, a Gothic tower house that restorers discovered behind a rococo facade in the 1960s.

➕ G7 ✉ Týnská 6 ☎ 224 827 022 🕐 Tue–Sun 10–6 🍴 Cafés and restaurants nearby 🚇 Staroměstská ✋ Moderate

KLEMENTINUM

Now the home of the National Library, this vast complex arranged around a series of courtyards was begun by the Jesuits in the late 16th century. A guided tour takes in some of the sumptuous interiors, including the Library Hall and Mirror Chapel, as well as the view from the Astronomical Tower.

➕ F7 ✉ Klementinum ☎ 221 663 111 🕐 Core hours: daily 2–6 🍴 Cafés and restaurants nearby 🚇 Staroměstská ✋ Moderate

STARÉ MĚSTO MORE TO SEE

The House of the Black Madonna is a cubist style building that houses the museum of Czech Cubism

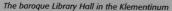

The baroque Library Hall in the Klementinum

KOSTEL PANNY MARIE PŘED TÝNEM (TÝN CHURCH)

Among the city's best-known landmarks is this Gothic church, whose twin towers stick up spikily behind the houses of Old Town Square. Inside are some fascinating tombs.

➕ G7 ✉ Enter from Staroměstská náměstí under the red address marker 604 🕐 Tue–Sat 10–1, 3–5 🍴 Cafés and restaurants nearby 🚇 Staroměstská

MUZEUM BEDŘICHA SMETANY (SMETANA MUSEUM)

The museum dedicated to the composer of "Vltava" is appropriately in a building that rises out of the river.

➕ E7 ✉ Novotného lávka 1 ☎ 222 220 082 🕐 Wed–Mon 10–5 🚇 Staroměstská 👣 Inexpensive

PALÁC KINSKÝCH (KINSKY PALACE)

Franz Kafka once attended school here and his father ran a haberdashery shop on the ground floor of this lovely rococo palace. In February 1948 the Communist coup d'etat was proclaimed from its balcony. The National Gallery exhibits its superb Asian art collections here.

➕ F7 ✉ Staroměstské náměstí 12 ☎ 224 810 758 🕐 Tue–Sun 10–6 🚇 Staroměstská 👣 Moderate

PRAŠNÁ BRÁNA (POWDER TOWER)

This famous gateway, with its chisel roof, was built as a ceremonial entrance to the Old Town. The climb to the top is worthwhile for the views.

➕ G7 ✉ Celetná 🕐 Apr–Sep daily 10–10; Oct, Mar 10–8; Nov–Feb 10–6 🚇 Náměstí Republiky 🚋 Tram 5, 14 to Náměstí Republiky 👣 Inexpensive

STAVOVSKÉ DIVADLO (ESTATES THEATER)

The venue that saw the première of Mozart's Don Giovanni in 1787 is a marvel of pristine neoclassical glory. Performances of Wolfgang's greatest hits can be enjoyed here.

➕ G7 ✉ Ovocný trh ☎ 224 901 448 🚇 Můstek

Powder Tower (Prašná Brána)

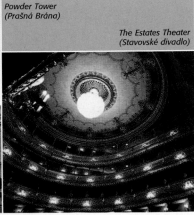

The Estates Theater (Stavovské divadlo)

Staré Město

Explore the crooked streets and squares of the Old Town on a walk that dips in and out of the Royal Way.

DISTANCE: 1.8km (1.2 miles) **ALLOW:** 1 hour

START

OBENCÍ DŮM
🔲 G7 🚇 Náměstí Republiky

1 From the Municipal House, go along Celetná, then turn right into the courtyard of No.17. This leads you into Štupartská, then into Malá Štupartská to the baroque façade of St. James's church.

2 Go back a few steps, turning right under the archway into Týn Court. Leave by the far entrance and go along the side of the Týn church into Old Town Square.

3 Leaving the Town Hall on your right, continue into Malé náměstí (Little Square). Turn right, then left into Mariánské náměstí (Marian Square).

4 Go left out of the square along Husová, passing on the left the Clam-Gallas palace with its muscular atlantes.

END

NOVOTNÉHO LÁVKA
🔲 E7 🚇 Staroměstská

8 Walk along the river toward Charles Bridge, turning left along the pier. End your walk by Smetana's statue outside the Smetana Museum.

7 Cross the square into the alleyway leading to Náprstkova; turn right. At the end of the street, go up the steps facing you on the landward side. Use the crossing to the left to cross the busy road to the riverside.

6 Continue in the same direction along Anenská, turning left into Anenské náměstí (Agnes Square). The square houses the Theater at the Balustrade, where Václav Havel began his theatrical career.

5 Make your way through the crowds thronging the Royal Way and continue a short distance along Husová, turning right into narrow Řetězová.

Shopping

AGHARTA

Jazz, jazz and more jazz on sale at the shop at this popular nightspot.
➕ F7 ✉ Železná 16
☎ 222 211 275 🚇 Můstek

ALMA ANTIQUE

This rambling, old-fashioned ground floor and basement establishment displays every conceivable kind of antique object.
➕ F7 ✉ Valentinská 7
☎ 224 813 991
🚇 Staroměstská

ANTIKVARIÁT KAREL KŘENEK

Old established antiquarian bookseller with an interesting selection of books, prints, old maps and lithographs.
➕ F8 ✉ Národní 20
☎ 222 314 734
🚇 Národní třída

ANTIKVARIÁT PAŘÍŽSKÁ

One of the few shops on this prestigious boulevard that does not deal in designer labels and fashion, with walls papered with antique maps and prints.
➕ F7 ✉ Pařížská 8
☎ 222 321 442
🚇 Staroměstská

ART DECO

Lots of glass, ceramics, clothing, jewelry and more from the 1920s and 1930s.
➕ F7 ✉ Michalská 21
☎ 224 223 076
🚇 Národní třída

ARTĚL

High-end, functional reproduction glassware inspired by avant-garde Czech designs of the 1920s and 1930s, as well as a unique selection of esoteric gift ideas. The shop is owned and operated by an American expat with a fine eye for value and lovable kitsch.
➕ G7 ✉ Celetná 29 (entrance on Rybná)
☎ 224 815 085
🚇 Náměstí Republiky

BOHEME

Smart and simple women's fashion, with an emphasis on high quality, well made, practical separates and all sorts of accessories.
➕ F6 ✉ Dušní 8 ☎ 224 813 840 🚇 Staroměstská

BOTANICUS

Organic products—soap, cosmetics, teas, herbs and spices—produced on a farm in Lysá nad Labem under the expert

---

REPRODUCTIONS

Genuine art nouveau objects can be expensive, cubist objects astronomically so. Superb, though far from cheap, reproductions of the latter can be found in an appropriate setting on the ground floor of the cubist Dům U Černé Matky Boží (House of the Black Madonna) at the eastern end of Celetná.
✉ Ovocný trh 19

---

supervision of a British specialist.
➕ F7 ✉ Týn 3 ☎ 234 767 446 🚇 Můstek

CELETNÁ CRYSTAL

Sells good-quality Bohemian glass from a selection of producers.
➕ G7 ✉ Celetná 15
☎ 222 324 022 🚇 Náměstí Republiky

COUNTRY LIFE

Healthy natural foods—elsewhere hard to find in this calorie-addicted city.
➕ F7 ✉ Melantrichova 15
☎ 224 213 366 🚇 Můstek

CULINARIA

Well-stocked international delicatessen. A particular boon for those more enthusiastic about the culinary products of the Mediterranean lands than those of Central Europe.
➕ F8 ✉ Skořepka 9
☎ 224 231 017 🚇 Národní třída/Můstek

DOROTHEUM

This branch of the long-established Vienna auction house has a fine range of antiques of all kinds. There may not be any bargains, but there are no rip-offs either.
➕ G7 ✉ Ovocný trh 2
☎ 224 222 001 🚇 Můstek or Náměstí Republiky

GALERIE PEITHNER-LICHTENFELS

Modern Czech and Austrian art, including works from the period between the two world

wars. The wide range of paintings, prints and sculptures makes a purchase possible for every pocket.

🚹 F7 ✉ Michalská 12
☎ 224 227 680 🚇 Můstek

GRANÁT

Bohemian garnets are world-famous and this factory shop boasts Prague's most varied selection.

🚹 G6 ✉ Dlouhá 28
☎ 222 315 612
🚇 Náměstí Republiky

HAVELSKÝ TRH

Atmospheric market for fruits, vegetables and souvenirs. Prices are generally lower than in the shops.

🚹 F7 ✉ Staré Město
🚇 Můstek

KNIHKUPECTVI TYNSKA

This arty bookstore specializes in antiquarian and Czech literature, with some English translations. Literary events are held in its basement café.

🚹 G7 ✉ Tynska
6–8 ☎ 224 827 807
🚇 Staroměstská, Můstek

MANUFAKTURA

Natural goods and traditional handicrafts, including linens, blankets, hand-dyed fabrics, wooden toys and Christmas ornaments. Also a range of cosmetics and hand-made soaps.

🚹 F7 ✉ Melantrichova 17
☎ 230 234 376 🚇 Můstek

MODERNISTA

Fans of cubist and early-Modern furniture design and decorative arts from the 1920s and 1930s will want to pop in at the Celetná showroom. Most of the affordable pieces here are reproductions, but there are some lovingly restored originals on offer, too.

🚹 G7 ✉ Celetná 12 ☎ 224 241 300 🚇 Staroměstská

PALLADIUM

Cleverly inserted into an historic barrack building, Prague's most up-to-date and lavish shopping mall is sited in the city center, just opposite the glorious art nouveau Obecní dům (Municipal House, ▷ 30–31). Here, countless shops coexist with a cocktail bar, a dance club and a vast food court.

Open daily till late.
🚹 G7 ✉ Náměstí Republiky 1 ☎ 225 770 250
🚇 Náměstí Republiky

QUBUS

A quirky design and gift shop, Qubus stocks a range of glassware and home furnishings in bold designs. This is the place to come if you're looking for something truly unique to take home as a souvenir.

🚹 G6 ✉ Rámová 3 ☎ 222 313 151 🚇 Staroměstská

TIMOURE ET GROUP

Chic and trendy women's fashion by two enterprising Czech graduates of the School of Applied Arts.

🚹 F/G6 ✉ V kolkovně 6
☎ 222 327 358
🚇 Staroměstská

TRUHLAR MARIONETY

For beautiful handmade wooden puppets and toys head to this specialist shop, which also runs its own theater and work-shop courses.

🚹 G7 ✉ Lužického sem. 5 ☎ 602 689 918
🚇 Staroměstská, Náměstí Republiky

VINO UNGELT

This well-stocked wine shop offers (for a fee) tastings from its huge range of Bohemian and Moravian vintages.

🚹 G7 ✉ Týn 7 ☎ 224 827 501 🚇 Náměstí Republiky

Entertainment and Nightlife

AGHARTA JAZZ CENTRUM

Cramped but enjoyable for local and international jazz, with cocktails and snacks. CD shop.
🚩 F7 ✉ Železná 16 ☎ 222 211 275 🚇 Můstek

DIVADLO IMAGE (IMAGE THEATER)

"Black light theater"shows, featuring dance, mime and music, performed in the dark.
🚩 F7 ✉ Pařížská 4 ☎ 222 329 191 🚇 Staroměstská

JAZZ LOUNGE U STARÉ PANÍ

Some of the best local musicians play in this central jazz club.
🚩 F7 ✉ Michalská 9 ☎ 605 285 211 🚇 Můstek

JAZZ 'N' BLUES CLUB UNGELT

More pub than club, this place hosts local and international talent.
🚩 G7 ✉ Týn 2 (enter from Týnská ulička) ☎ 224 895 748 🚇 Staroměstská

KARLOVY LÁZNĚ

Self-proclaimed Central Europe's biggest club gets going around 11pm until dawn most nights.
🚩 E7/8 ✉ Smetanovo nábřeží 198 ☎ 222 220 502 🚇 Staroměstská

KLEMENTINUM

This vast complex (▷ 35) hosts chamber concerts in its Hall of Mirrors (Zrcadlová síň).
🚩 F7 ✉ Entrances

at Karlova 1, Mariánské náměsti and Křižovnické náměstí ☎ 222 220 879 🚇 Staroměstská

NÁRODNÍ DIVADLO MARIONET (NATIONAL MARION-ETTE THEATER)

Adaptations of operas are among the attractions, and there are matinees for youngsters.
🚩 F7 ✉ Žatecká 1 ☎ 224 819 322 🚇 Staroměstská

ROXY

Unusual underground establishment that has DJs and live acts of every conceivable stripe, including stars of world music.
🚩 G6 ✉ Dlouhá 33 ☎ 602 691 015 🚇 Staroměstská

RUDOLFINUM

The Dvořák Hall of this neo-Renaissance hall

CINEMA

Czechs love the movies—both their own domestic productions as well as Hollywood blockbusters. Several of the old movie houses have survived. Look for the Lucerna cinema at the Lucerna shopping passage (▷ 58) and the Svůtozor cinema, which often plays Czech movies with English subtitles. The best multiplex is Cinema City in the Slovanský dům shopping mall (▷ 58). Check the *Prague Post* for full details.

located on the Vltava is the home of the Czech Philharmonic Orchestra. The Little (or Suk) Hall is used for chamber concerts.
🚩 F6 ✉ Alšovo nátřeží 12 ☎ 227 059 227 🚇 Staroměstská

SMETANOVA SÍŇ (SMETANA HALL)

www.fok.cz
Part of the sumptuously decorated Municipal House (▷ 30), and home of the first-class Prague Symphony Orchestra.
🚩 G7 ✉ Náměstí Republiky 5 ☎ 222 002 336 🚇 Náměstí Republiky

STAVOVSKÉ DIVADLO (ESTATES THEATER)

The spectacular neoclassical auditorium of the Estates Theater, with five tiers of box seats, is a wonderful setting for opera. Performances are at 7.30pm, with matinees on weekends. Also ▷ 36.
🚩 G7 ✉ Ovocný trh 1 ☎ 224 901 448 🚇 Můstek

TA FANTASTIKA

Another spectacle based on the black light fusion of dance, mime and music—a spin-off from the hugely successful Laterna Magika. The stage also hosts pop musicals starring local idols.
🚩 F7 ✉ Karlova 8 ☎ 222 221 366 🚇 Staroměstská

Restaurants

PRICES

Prices are approximate, based on a 3-course meal for one person.

£££ over 800Kč
££ 400Kč–800Kč
£ under 400Kč

AMICI MIEI (££)

Enjoy impeccable Italian food and service in this Josefov restaurant. Seafood specialties and an extensive cellar stocked with an array of imported wines.

✚ G6 ✉ Vězeňská 5
☎ 224 816 688 🚇 Tram 17 to Pravnická fakulta

BAKESHOP (£–££)

Possibly the best bakery and sandwich shop in Central Europe stocks a wide variety of freshly made soups and sandwiches, plus innovative salads. Try the tempting selection of cakes, cookies and brownies.

✚ G6 ✉ Kozí 1 ☎ 222 316 823 🚇 Staroměstská

BELLEVUE (£££)

If dining with a view is what you're after, you can't do any better than this. Request a window table looking out over the Vltava and Prague Castle in the distance. Expect a great interior and topnotch international cuisine.

✚ F6 ✉ Smetanovo nábřeží 18 ☎ 222 221 443 🚇 Staroměstská 🚋 Tram 6, 9, 17, 18 to Národní divaldo

CHEZ MARCEL (£–££)

This comfy café/restaurant serves up typical French bistro fare. Popular among expats.

✚ G6 ✉ Haštalská 12
☎ 222 315 676 🚋 Tram 5, 8, 14 to Dlouhá třída

COTTOCRUDO (£££)

This riverside restaurant at the Four Seasons Hotel (▷ 112) gives traditional Italian cooking a modern stir. There is a cocktail bar and DJs on Thursday and Friday nights.

✚ F7 ✉ Veleslavínova 2a ☎ 221 426 880 🚇 Staroměstská

KING SOLOMON (£££)

Good kosher food and a lovely winter garden in the heart of the Josefov.

✚ F7 ✉ Široka 8, Josefov ☎ 224 818 752 🚇 Staroměstská

KOLKOVNA (£–££)

This updated take on the traditional pub, near Old Town Square, serves Czech staples along with pastas and salads. Great

VEGGIE REVOLUTION

Before 1989, vegetarians venturing to Prague were liable to be served endless omelettes, perhaps with extra dumplings. Czechs still like their rich and hearty meat-based dishes, but the quality and range of vegetarian offerings continue to improve.

for groups, but be sure to reserve in advance.

✚ F6 ✉ V Kolkovně 8
☎ 224 819 701
🚇 Staroměstská

LOKAL (£)

For the budget-conscious and those able to read a menu in Czech (the staff will help), this very long dining room serves up sublimely ordinary food, the trick being that everything is made from the best ingredients.

✚ G6 ✉ Dlouhà 33
☎ 222 316 265 🚇 Náměstí Republiky

MAITREA (£)

The finest meat-free fare served in a calm and contemplative ambience on two floors.

✚ G7 ✉ Týnská ulička 6
☎ 221 711 631
🚇 Staroměstská or Náměstí Republiky

PIZZA NUOVA (£–££)

If you're visiting with young children, it's hard not to like an all-you-can-eat pizza and pasta menu, with an adjoining supervized play room for small children. The pizzas are authentic—from a Naples recipe. The antipasto buffet is very good value.

✚ G7 ✉ Revolucní 1
☎ 221 803 308
🚇 Náměstí Republiky

PLZEŇSKÁ RESTAURACE (££)

In the basement of the Municipal House

(▷ 30) is this art nouveau designer's idea of what a Bohemian beer hall should look like. The food is standard pub fare such as goulash.

➕ G7 ✉ Náměstí Republiky 5 ☎ 222 002 780 Ⓜ Náměstí Republiky

POTREFENÁ HUSA (£)

This is a branch of the "Wounded Goose"— bright, cheerful and very contemporary bars with satisfying Czech and international food.

➕ F7 ✉ Platnéřská 9 ☎ 224 813 892 Ⓜ Staroměstská

SAGE (£££)

Sumptuous fish and seafood restaurant (formerly Rybí Trh) in the enchanting Týn Court.

➕ G7 ✉ Týn 5 ☎ 224 895 447 Ⓜ Staroměstská or Náměstí Republiky

SLAVIA (£)

This classic Central European café, once the haunt of dissident intellectuals, has a superb view over the Vltava. Live piano music nightly.

➕ E8 ✉ Smetanovo nábřeží 2 ☎ 224 218 493 Ⓜ Národní třída

LE TERROIR (£££)

This atmospheric establishment offers the very finest in French-inspired cuisine together with wines from an exceptionally well-stocked cellar.

➕ F7 ✉ Vejvodová 1 ☎ 222 220 260 Ⓜ Národní třída

U MEDVÍDKŮ (£)

Budvar, from the town of České Budějovice in southern Bohemia, is probably the best-known Bohemian beer apart from Pilsener. Sample it on tap, in the garden, in summer at this beerhall and former brewery. Their X-Beer is claimed to be the strongest in the country at 11.8 percent.

➕ F8 ✉ Na Perštýně 7 ☎ 224 211 916 Ⓜ Národní třída

U MODRÉ KACHNIČKY II (££)

The "Blue Duckling II" is an offshoot of the original Malá Strana restaurant (▷ 94). Both offer a sophisticated take on traditional Bohemian cuisine, featuring game dishes.

TURKISH COFFEE

Global coffee culture has conquered Prague, but it's still possible to get served a traditional *turecká káva*. This is Czech-style Turkish coffee—that is, hot water poured right over ground coffee. Invariably served in a piping-hot glass with no handle. Be sure to stop swallowing—that is before you disturb the deposit of coffee grounds at the bottom of the cup.

➕ F7 ✉ Michalská 16 ☎ 224 213 418 Ⓜ Můstek

U VEJVODŮ (£)

This old pub blends preserved architectural styles from Gothic to art nouveau, and offers a similarly eclectic range of good food, beer and live music from Bohemia.

➕ F7 ✉ Jilská 4 ☎ 224 219 999 Ⓜ Národní třída

V ZÁTIŠÍ (£££)

One of the first gourmet establishments to open up after the Velvet Revolution, "Still Life" continues to offer some of the finest food in town, specializing in Bohemian and Indian cuisine.

➕ E7 ✉ Liliová 1 ☎ 222 221 155 🚋 Tram 17, 18 to Karlovy lazně

YAMI (£–££)

Succulent and freshly cooked sushi in this cozy little Japanese-Korean fusion restaurant. Closed on Mondays.

➕ G6 ✉ Masná 1051 ☎ 222 312 756 Ⓜ Staroměstská

ZLATÁ PRAHA (£££)

High up on the ninth floor of the Communist-era Intercontinental Hotel, with stunning views over the Old Town, "Golden Prague" pulls out all the stops to give an unforgettable dining experience.

➕ F6 ✉ Pařížská 30 ☎ 296 630 522 🚋 Tram 17, 18 to Pravnická fakulta

Nové Město

Prague's commercial heart beats strongly in the New Town. The district is focused on a series of squares; foremost is Václavské náměstí, with Národní muzeum and the statue of Good King Wenceslas.

Vltava

ŠTĚPÁNSKÁ

NÁBŘEŽÍ LUDVÍKA SVOBODY   TĚŠNOVSKÝ TUNEL

Na Františku

Přístav prům   Lannova   min
a obchodu   dopravy
                            HOLBOVA
Poštovní
muzeum   KLIMENTSKÁ   KE
                                          ŠTVANIC
Klimentská   Petrská   Těšnov
Soukenická   Barvířská   Florenc Sokolovská

Truhlářská   Na poříčí   Bílá
                              labuť
                    Na poříčí **Muzeum**   Florenc
        Na poříčí   **hlavního**   KŘIŽÍKOVA
Štěpánský   **města Prahy**   Hudební
dům   Florenc divadlo

            Masarykovo
            nádraží   Náměstí
            V celnici   Republiky
Muchovo   **ŽEL ST MASARYKOVO**
muzeum   **NÁDRAŽÍ**
sv Jindřich Hybernská   Hybernská   HUSITSKÁ

Muzeum   Hlavní
komunismu   nádraží   Seifertova

Panny   Můstek   Bredov
Marie   palác   Dlážďkův
sněžné   Dačický palác
div   **Václavské**   **HLAVNÍ**
Adria   **náměstí**   **NÁDRAŽÍ**
Františkánská
    zahrada   Opletalova
div Rokoko   WILSONOVA
U Hájků
div ABC   Petschkův
Kalich   palác   Státní
     Vodičkova   opera
Obvodní   Nová budova
úřad   Národního muzea
Navrátilova   sv Václav
div V Řeznické   Vinohradská
Řeznická   **Národní**
ZITNA   **muzeum**   Římská
            ŽITNA   Čelakovského
                    MEZIBRANSKÁ   sady
            Na Rybníčku   ANGLICKÁ
Malá   sv Štěpán Hálkova
Štěpánská   Mikovcova
JEČNÁ   IP Pavlova
    Štěpánská   náměstí IP Pavlova
            JEČNÁ I P Pavlova Jugoslávská
sv Ignác
NOVÉ   I P Pavlova
MĚSTO
nemocnice   RUMUNSKÁ
            muzeum
            A Dvořáka
    svatá   Tyršova
    Kateřina   Fügnerovo
            Kateřinská nám
    psychiat   Apolinářská   LEGEROVA
    klinika
univerzity Karlovy Žitkovská Wenzigova
sv Apolinář porodnice
Albertov   B Němcové
    Albertov
Muzeum P Marie
policie ČR Horská
Albertov Hlavova
Horská
        Folimanka
    NUSELSKÝ MOST
        SEKANINOVA
Ostrčilovo Oldřichova
náměstí   Svatoplukova
        JAROMÍROVA
P Maria
sv Martina
        SLAVOJOVA
Ludmila
ústav
G   **H**   **J**

Muchovo muzeum

Advertising poster (left); detail of a window sculpture (right)

HIGHLIGHTS

● Sarah Bernhardt Gismonda poster
● Moravian Teachers' Choir poster
● Re-created Paris studio
● Biographical film

Best known for his posters of languorous Parisian lovelies advertising everything from champagne to cigarettes, the art nouveau artist Alfons Mucha was a proud Czech patriot whose later work celebrated his country's independence.

Alfons's vision Alfons Mucha (1860–1939) was an émigré Czech who first found fame in Paris when he created a sensation with a stunning poster of the actress Sarah Bernhardt. Mucha was an idealist who hoped that art nouveau would break down the barriers between high art and everyday design. After his return to Prague, he worked on a variety of projects, from decorating the interiors of the Obecní dům (▷ 30) to designing stamps and banknotes for the new Czechoslovak Republic and stained glass for St. Vitus's Cathedral.

Museum exhibits Housed in the 18th-century Kaunic Palace, this museum shows off Mucha memorabilia, as well as drawings, paintings and sculpture. It also houses an atmospheric re-creation of the Paris studio that the artist shared with Rodin and Gauguin. In his later years, Mucha devoted himself to a sequence of 20 immense canvases depicting high points in the history of the Czechs and other Slav peoples. The paintings were intended to be put on permanent display in the capital, and since 2012 they have been on display at the National Gallery's Veletržní palác (Veletržní Palace, ▷ 100–101), as the Slav Epic series.

Národní divadlo

Even if the thought of a classical play performed in Czech doesn't enthrall you, don't miss the National Theater. It is, perhaps, the greatest of Prague's collective works of art, decorated by the finest artists of the age.

National drama Plays in Prague were still performed in German in the mid-19th century. Money to build a specifically Czech theater was collected from 1849 onward, without support from Habsburg-dominated official-dom. The foundation stone was laid in 1868 with much festivity, then in 1881, shortly after the gala opening, the building burned down. Undiscouraged, the populace rallied, and by 1883 it had been completely rebuilt. The opening was celebrated with a grand gala performance of the opera *Libuše* by Smetana, a passionate supporter of the building's project.

Expanded ambition The National Theater stands at the New Town end of Most Legií (Legions Bridge), its bulk carefully angled to fit into the streetscape and not diminish the view to Petřín Hill on the far bank. It was given a long-deserved restoration in time for its centenary, and when it reopened in 1983 it had gained a piazza and three annexes, whose architecture has been much maligned, the least unkind comment being that the buildings seem to be clad in bubble-wrap. Prague's popular multimedia show Laterna Magika (▷ 59) performs in one of the buildings, the Nová scéna.

THE BASICS

www.narodni-divadlo.cz
🔢 E8
✉ Národní 2
☎ 224 901 448
🕐 Box office: daily 10–6
🍴 Bar
🚊 Tram 6, 9, 17, 18, 21, 22 to Národní divadlo
♿ Few
🎫 Opera tickets: inexpensive–expensive

HIGHLIGHTS

● Bronze troikas above the entrance loggia
● Star-patterned roof of the dome
● Frescoes in the foyer by Mikoláš Aleš
● Painted ceiling of the auditorium, by František Ženíšek
● Painted stage curtain by Vojtěch Hynais
● View of the building from Střelecký Island
● Any performance of an opera from the Czech repertoire

Národní muzeum

The spacious three-floor staircase (left); sculpture outside the museum (below)

THE BASICS

www.nm.cz
- H9
- Václavské náměstí 68
- 224 497 111
- May–Sep daily 10–6; Oct–Apr 9–5. Closed first Tue of month
- Café
- Muzeum
- Few
- Moderate

HIGHLIGHTS

● The 70m (230ft) dome
● Allegorical sculptures on the museum steps
● Socialist-Realist sculpture at the front of new building

A much-needed restoration has caused the closure of the National Museum since 2011, but this enormous city landmark is due to reopen in June 2015.

Top building With its gilded dome crowning the rise at the top of Václavské náměstí (Wenceslas Square, ▷ 50), Prague's National Museum provides a grand finale to the capital's most important street. The neo-Renaissance building was completed in 1891, and at the time was as much an object of pride to the Czech populace as the Národní divadlo (National Theater, ▷ 47). Such is its presence that some visitors have mistaken it for the parliament building, as did the Soviet gunner who raked its facade with machine-gun fire in August 1968.

The new building During the renovation, most of the museum's vast collections have been kept in store. Some, however, remain on show, together with temporary exhibitions, in the neighboring building, the former Federal Parliament of Czechoslovakia. Incongruously straddling the old Stock Exchange, this uncompromising Communist-era edifice also stages temporary exhibitions. Eventually it is planned to link new to old by means of a pedestrian plaza; exhibition space will be nearly doubled. A plaque on the north wall of the new building honors Alexander Dubček, the hero of the 1968 Prague Spring and first Speaker of the post-communist Parliament.

**Rising high above the River Vltava is
Vyšehrad (High Castle), where the
soothsaying Princess Libuše foresaw
the founding of Prague, and where she
married her ploughman swain, Přemysl.**

Romantic rock Beneath Vyšehrad's
19th-century neo-Gothic Church of St. Peter
and St. Paul are the remains of a far earlier,
Romanesque church that once served the royal
court. But it was in the 19th century, with the rise
of Romantic ideas about history and nationhood,
that poets, playwrights and painters celebrated
the great fortress-rock, elaborating the story of
Libuše. Most of their efforts have been forgotten,
though Smetana's "Vyšehrad", part of his glorious tone-poem *Má Vlast*, remains popular. The
nation's great and good have been buried in the
National Cemetery (or Pantheon) at Vyšehrad
since the late 19th century. Smetana himself is
here, and fellow composer Dvořák. On the lawns
nearby are freestanding sculptures of Libuše
and other legendary figures by Josef Václav
Myslbek, the creator of the St. Wenceslas statue
in Wenceslas Square.

Vltava views Everyone driving along the
main riverside highway has to pay homage to
Vyšehrad, as the road and tram tracks twist
and turn and then tunnel through the high
rock protruding into the Vltava. In the 1920s
the whole hilltop was turned into a public
park, with wonderful views up and down the
river (▷ 52).

THE BASICS

www.praha-vysehrad.cz
✚ F12
✉ Information area: V
Pevnosti 159/56, Vyšehrad
☎ 241 410 348
◉ Prague Fortifications
Museum: Apr–Oct daily
9.30–6; Nov–Mar 9.30–5.
Cemetery: Apr–Oct 8–6;
Nov–Mar 8–5
🍴 Restaurant
Ⓜ Vyšehrad
🚃 Trams 3, 7, 16, 17 to
Výtoň then steep uphill
walk
♿ Fair
✋ Park and cemetery:
free; Museum: inexpensive

HIGHLIGHTS

● National Cemetery graves
and the Slavín mausoleum
● St. Martin's Rotunda
● Cihelná brána (Brick Gate),
with Prague Fortifications
Museum
● Ramparts walk
● Neo-Gothic Kostel sv Petra
a Pavla (Church of St. Peter
and St. Paul)

Václavské náměstí

HIGHLIGHTS

- St. Wenceslas statue, Josef Myslbek (1912)
- Arcades of the Lucerna Palace
- Hotel Evropa, completed 1905 (No. 25)
- 1920s Functionalist Baťa and Lindt buildings (Nos. 4, 6)
- Ambassador, late art nouveau hotel of 1912 (No. 5)
- Memorial to Jan Palach
- 1950s Soviet-style Jalta Hotel (No. 45)
- Former Bank of Moravia of 1916 (Nos. 38–40)
- Art nouveau Peterka building of 1900 (No. 12)
- Koruna Palace of 1914 (No. 1)

Despite its sometimes rather seedy air, Wenceslas Square is still the place where the city's heart beats most strongly, and to meet someone "beneath the horse" (the Wenceslas statue) remains a thrill.

When is a square not a square? When it's a boulevard. "Václavák", 750m (820 yards) long, slopes gently up to the imposing facade of the National Museum (▷ 48). Just down the slope stands the statue of "Good King" Wenceslas on his sprightly steed, a good place for a rendezvous at any time of day and night.

History in the making Many dramas of modern times have been played out in Wenceslas Square. The new state of Czechoslovakia was proclaimed here in 1918, and in 1939 German

Clockwise from far left: Looking down Wenceslas Square; statue of Wenceslas on an upside-down horse, Lucerna Palace; equestrian statue of Wenceslas; classical statues support a bay window on Václavské náměstí; sgraffito facade on a building on Wenceslas Square; café of the Evropa Hotel; Wiehluv dum (exterior views)

tanks underlined the republic's demise. In 1968, more tanks arrived—this time to crush the Prague Spring of Alexander Dubček. To protest at the Soviet occupation, Jan Palach burned himself to death here in 1969, and in 1989 Dubček and Václav Havel waved from the balcony of No. 36 as Czechs crowded here to celebrate the collapse of Communism.

Museum of modern architecture The procession of buildings lining both sides of the square, from the resplendent art nouveau Hotel Evropa to the elegant Functionalist Bat'a Store, tells the story of the Czech contribution to 20th-century architecture and design. More intriguing are the arcades that burrow deep into the buildings, creating a labyrinth of boutiques, entertainment venues, cafés and cinemas.

THE BASICS

➕ G–H8
✉ Václavské náměstí
🍴 Many restaurants and cafés
🚇 Můstek or Muzeum
♿ Fair

TIP

● Wenceslas Square is a popular place for people-watching. Head to one of the terrace cafés on its east side, which catch the midday and afternoon sun.

Vltava Boat Trip

HIGHLIGHTS

● Frank Gehry's "Dancing Building"
● Charles Bridge from beneath
● Art nouveau Čech Bridge

TIP

● Check the weather forecast and plan your cruise for a fine day. If you sit on the open deck, you will be exposed to the sun—so don't forget to wear sunscreen.

A cruise is a wonderful way to see Prague from a different angle. Some of the city's bridges are works of art, and there are many other fascinating river sights immortalized by Bedřich Smetana.

National river The Vltava (sometimes known by its German name of Moldau) rises high in the hills along the Austrian border. Flowing north into the Elbe (Labe in Czech) some 40km (25 miles) downstream from Prague, its waters eventually discharge into the North Sea. Mostly tranquil, the river's mood can change suddenly; its banks have often burst, and in 1890 it swept away several of the arches of Charles Bridge. Dams upstream were supposed to have tamed it, but failed to prevent the disastrous flood of August 2002, when much of

Clockwise from left: River boats cruise the Vltava; Slavonic Island and an old water-tower; fishermen patiently wait for their first catch of the day; color-washed facades line the riverbank, with the towers of St. Vitus's Cathedral behind

Malá Strana, Smíchov, Karlín and the cellars of Staré Město were inundated. Despite such incidents, it's the most loved of Czech rivers.

Riverside delights Several operators run boat trips down the Vltava that are an especially fun way to spend an afternoon or evening. Most of the boats leave from the embankment just below Čechův most (the Čech bridge, near the Hotel Intercontinental) and cruise upstream to beyond Charles Bridge and on to near Vyšehrad before turning back. Cruises run year-around, though summer is obviously a better bet for suitable weather and offers more of a choice among different cruises. The main operator is Evropská vodní doprava (EVD) (▷ The Basics panel), but tours can be booked through many different travel agencies.

THE BASICS

Evropská vodní doprava
www.evd.cz
✉ Quay at Cechuv most
☎ 224 810 030
🕐 Year-round, though more frequent departures in summer
✋ Moderate–expensive
❓ Useful websites for cruises:
www.pragueexperience.com
www.cruise-prague.cz
www.myczechrepublic.com

More to See

KARLOVO NÁMĚSTÍ

Karlovo náměstí (Charles Square) is more of a park than a square, and a useful resting place in this spread-out part of town.

✚ F9

MUZEUM HLAVNÍHO MĚSTA PRAHY (CITY MUSEUM)

www.muzeumprahy.cz

This late 19th-century building contains exhibits telling the story of Prague's evolution from the earliest times. The star is a scale model of the city as it was in the 1820s and 1830s. Most of the extensive collections are in storage, but selections are shown in rotation.

✚ J6 ✉ Na Poříčí 52, north Nové Město ☎ 224 816 773 🕐 Tue–Sun 9–6 🚇 Florenc ✋ Moderate

MUZEUM KOMUNISMU

www.museumofcommunism.com

The Museum of Communism is a private venture, which has attracted much controversy. The museum contrasts Communism's Utopian dreams with the grim reality of empty shops, meaningless slogans and pervasive policing. An upbeat note is struck at the end, however, with a short film about the Velvet Revolution, which brought an end to the oppressive regime.

✚ G7 ✉ Na Příkopě 10 ☎ 224 212 966 🕐 Daily 9–9 🚇 Můstek ✋ Moderate, child under 10 free with paying adult

MUZEUM POLICIE ČR (POLICE MUSEUM)

www.muzeumpolicie.cz

This museum recovered quickly from the collapse of the old order in 1989 and gives an upbeat account of Czech policing, with lots of gore and weaponry on show in what was once a monastery.

✚ G11 ✉ Ke Karlovu 1 ☎ 224 922 183 🕐 Tue–Sun 10–5 🚇 I P Pavlova or Vyšehrad ✋ Inexpensive

PANNY MARIE SNĚŽNÉ

http://pms.ofm.cz

The great Gothic Church of Our Lady of the Snows was intended by

Novoměstská radnice (Town Hall) on Karlovo náměstí

Carved figures inside the Church of Our Lady of the Snows

Emperor Charles IV to rival St. Vitus's Cathedral and to dominate the skyline of the New Town. However, the Hussite Troubles ended building, and only the chancel was completed. The best view of the exterior is from the Franciscans' Garden. The interior demonstrates both Gothic mastery of space and baroque determination not to be outdone.

✚ G8 ✉ Jungmannovo náměstí 18
☎ 222 246 243 🕐 Daily 7–7 (no visiting during Mass) Ⓜ Můstek 🚋 Tram 6, 9, 18, 21, 22 to Národní třída 💷 Free

POŠTOVNÍ MUZEUM

www.postovnimuzeum.cz

The Postal Museum houses the national collection of stamps and postal memorabilia in a 16th-century building with original painted interiors. The emphasis is on stamps from Czechoslovakia and its successor republics, but there's much else besides.

✚ G6 ✉ Nové mlýny 2 ☎ 222 312 006
🕐 Tue–Sun 9–12, 1–5 🚋 Tram 8, 14, 26 to Dlouhá třída 💷 Inexpensive

SVATÉHO CYRILA A METODĚJE

On 18 June 1942, the baroque Church of Saints Cyril and Methodius was where the Czechoslovak parachutists who had assassinated Reichsprotektor Reinhard Heydrich made their last stand. After their hiding place in the crypt was betrayed by a former comrade, they valiantly held SS troops at bay with a hail of bullets for several hours. Finally, the fire brigade was ordered to flush them out by pumping water into the crypt. Rather than fall into the hands of a merciless enemy, the defenders used their last bullets on themselves. Their heroism, and that of the churchmen who hid them, is commemorated by a plaque outside the church and by displays in the crypt itself.

✚ F9 ✉ Resslova 9 ☎ 224 920 686
🕐 Mar–Oct Tue–Sun 9–5; Nov–Feb Tue–Sat 9–5 💷 Moderate Ⓜ Karlovo náměstí
🚋 Tram 3, 4, 6, 7, 10, 14, 16, 17, 18, 21, 22, 23, 24 to Karlovo náměstí

A display in the museum housed in the Vila Amerika (▷ 60)

Exterior of the Státní Opera Praha (Opera House; ▷ 60)

The Old and New

This route takes you along the bustling boulevards laid out along the dividing line between the Old and New Towns.

DISTANCE: 1.75km (just over a mile) **ALLOW:** 45 minutes

START ....

OBECNÍ DŮM
🚩 G7 🚇 Náměstí Republiky

① Turn right and walk along Na příkopě. Now one of Prague's main shopping streets, it divides—or links—the Old and New Towns.

② Pause to look inside the ornate Živnostenská banka (Na příkopě 20), built in 1896. In contrast on the north side of the street is the sober Komerční banka of 1908.

③ The point where Na příkopě joins Wenceslas Square is called Můstek, or "Little Bridge".

④ Walk up the right-hand side of Wenceslas Square (▷ 50–51), and turn right into the Alfa passage (Václavské náměstí 28) into the landscaped Franciscans' Garden.

END ....

NÁRODNI DIVADLO
🚩 E8 🚇 Tram: 6, 9, 17, 18, 21, 22

⑧ Národní třída ends at the Národní divadlo (National Theater, ▷ 47). Opposite the building is the famous Café Slavia.

⑦ Continue along the left-hand side of Národní třída. In the arcade of No.16 look for the little memorial commemorating the victims of police brutality during the 1989 Velvet Revolution.

⑥ Go past the statue of Josef Jungmann into Národní třída (National Avenue), laid out like Na příkopě along the line of the Old Town ramparts.

⑤ Leave the garden via the far corner into Jungmannovo náměstí.

NOVÉ MĚSTO WALK

56

Shopping

ACADEMIA
Good variety of photography books, travel guides, cookbooks and literature in English.
✚ G8 ✉ Václavské náměstí 34 ☎ 221 403 840
Ⓜ Můstek

ANTIKVARIÁT GALLERIE MŮSTEK
This old-established firm in the arcade of the Adria Palace is a typical example of the Prague *antikvariát* (antiquarian bookshop), with not just books but an intriguing selection of maps, prints and a range of ephemera.
✚ G8 ✉ Národní třída 40
☎ 224 949 587 Ⓜ Můstek or Národní třída

BAT'A
An iconic early 20th-century building, the sleek Bat'a store on Wenceslas Square sells the world-famous Czech company's shoes on several floors.
✚ G8 ✉ Václavské náměstí 6 ☎ 221 088 478
Ⓜ Můstek

BISTRO DELI & BAKERY
www.bistrodeli.cz
This bright little deli bakes some of the tastiest bread, cakes and pastries in town, with freshly made sandwiches to take away; it also has a few tables at the back where breakfast and snacks are served throughout the day.
✚ G9 ✉ Štěpánská 20
☎ 230 234 211 Ⓜ Muzeum

BONTONLAND
This is reputedly the biggest music shop in Central Europe. The pop and rock section is vast, classical hardly less so. And there are DVDs and games galore. It is in the labyrinthine basement of the Koruna Palace at the corner of Wenceslas Square and Na příkopě.
✚ G6/7 ✉ Václavské náměstí 1 ☎ 224 473 080
Ⓜ Můstek

CELLARIUS
In the Lucerna arcade off Wenceslas Square (▷ 58), this well-stocked shop sells wines from around the world as well as from the vineyards of Bohemia and Moravia.
✚ G8 ✉ Štěpánská 61
☎ 224 210 979 Ⓜ Můstek

MALL MAGIC

The arrival of Western-style malls has transformed the shopping scene in Prague. With their bright and shiny, if not innovative, architecture and interior design they are a world away from the sterile and lifeless state-run department stores in the Communist era. As a visitor, you probably won't want to spend too much time at the malls, but they are still useful places to pick up items you might have left at home. The biggest mall in Prague is Palladium at Náměstí Republiky 1 (▷ 39), opposite the Municipal House.

CENTRUM FOTOŠKODA
A paradise for camera buffs, stocking every possible kind of photographic equipment (new and secondhand) as well as books and magazines.
✚ G8 ✉ Vodičkova 37
☎ 222 929 029 Ⓜ Můstek

DŮM PORCELÁNU
Very good selection of Czech-made porcelain from outlets in Western Bohemia at prices that are aimed at the local market—not tourists.
✚ H9 ✉ Jugoslávská 16
☎ 221 505 320
Ⓜ I P Pavlova

ELAZAR
The Prague outlet of this venerable maker of fine clothes and accessories in fur and leather is on the ground floor of the Černá Růže arcade.
✚ G7 ✉ Na příkopě 12
☎ 221 014 330 Ⓜ Můstek

GLOBE BOOKSTORE AND COFFEEHOUSE
A congenial home-from-home for Americans and anyone hungry for literature in English, as well as light meals.
✚ F9 ✉ Pštrossova 6
☎ 224 934 203 Ⓜ Národní třída or Karlovo náměstí

HODINÁŘSTVÍ MATOUŠ
Beautiful antique clocks and watches.
✚ F8 ✉ Mikulandská 10
☎ 224 930 172
Ⓜ Národní třída

KIWI

A travel agency, Kiwi also sells a comprehensive range of maps and guides to the Czech Republic and beyond. Hanging on the walls in the basement is a fascinating collection of excellent maps.

✚ G8 ✉ Jungmannova 23 ☎ 222 230 107 Ⓜ Národní třída

KLIMENT

Czechs are known for their love of music, from classical to pop, and here is where they buy their instruments. One of the best selections in the city.

✚ G8 ✉ Jungmannova 17 ☎ 224 213 966 Ⓜ Můstek

LUCERNA PASSAGE

How shopping centers used to look in the 1920s—fun, elegant and filled with character. There are not actually many shops here aside from some small gift stores, boutiques and a wine shop, but that makes it all the better. There's a big period-piece cinema, two excellent cafés and one of the best-known music clubs in the city. Worth seeking out.

✚ G7 ✉ Štěpánská 61 ☎ 224 224 537 Ⓜ Můstek or Muzeum

MINERALIA

Part jewelry store, part museum, this huge establishment claims to have the largest mineral collection in Central Europe, selling everything from gemstone key rings to meteorites.

✚ H7 ✉ Havlickova 3, Malá Strana ☎ 606 503 053 Ⓜ Náměstí Republiky

MOSER

A palatial first-floor outlet for the fine crystal and porcelain made in Carlsbad (Karlový Vary), along with porcelain from Meissen and Herend. No bargains, but objects of the highest quality are beautifully displayed here.

✚ G7 ✉ Na Příkopě 12 ☎ 224 211 293 Ⓜ Můstek or Náměstí Republiky

MY

Tesco's flagship downtown department store, with six floors and a useful supermarket in the basement.

✚ F8 ✉ Národní trída 26 ☎ 221 003 111 Ⓜ Národní třída

MYSLIVOST

This shop caters to that army of Czechs who love the outdoor life. Unusual weatherproof wear and much else.

✚ G8 ✉ Jungmannova 25 ☎ 224 949 017 Ⓜ Národní třída

PALÁC KNIH LUXOR

There's no reason to dispute the claim of the "Palace of Books" to be the biggest in the country. Descend to the basement for books in English and other foreign languages. The firm has another sizeable store in the Nový Smíchov mall.

✚ G8 ✉ Václavské náměstí 41 ☎ 296 110 384 Ⓜ Můstek or Muzeum

SLOVANSKÝ DŮM

Another shopping mall—just down the street from Palladium—but much more relaxed and manageable. Check out the restaurant Kogo and the multiplex cinema.

✚ G7 ✉ Na Příkopě 22 Ⓜ Můstek

ZLATÝ KŘÍŽ

Crowds of locals throng "the Golden Cross" at lunch because it has what is probably the widest range of *obložené chlebíčky* (open sandwiches) in Prague, as well as cakes and drinks. You can stand at the buffet and consume your finds or take them away and picnic in the nearby Franciscans' Garden.

✚ G8 ✉ Jungmannovo náměstí 19 Ⓜ Můstek or Národní třída

ČERNÉ DIVADLO JIŘÍHO SRNEC (JIŘÍ SRNEC BLACK THEATER)

Legends of magic Prague presented in multimedia format. Jiří Srnec was the originator of black light cinema some 40 years ago. The show features a cast of clowns, acrobats and wizards, in a flight of fantasy that will delight youngsters and the young at heart.

➕ F8 ✉ Na Příkopě 10, ☎ 774 547 475 🚇 Můstek

DIVADLO ARCHA (ARCHA THEATER)

The Archa Theater reaches out to non-Czech speakers with a fascinating avant-garde agenda of drama, dance, music and multimedia productions. Tickets for most shows are relatively inexpensive and highly sought after—so make reservations well in advance.

➕ H6 ✉ Na Poříčí 26 ☎ 221 716 111 🚇 Náměstí Republiky

DIVADLO HYBERNIA

In a former monastery, this theater is aimed squarely at the tourist market, staging popular ballets and classical highlights concerts. The performances are of a high standard and a fun evening is virtually guaranteed.

➕ G7 ✉ Náměstí Republiky 4 ☎ 221 419 416/420 🚇 Náměstí Republiky

DIVADLO MINOR (MINOR THEATER)

This well-known puppetry and drama ensemble puts on a varied schedule designed to appeal to children.

➕ G9 ✉ Vodičkova 6 ☎ 222 231 351 🚇 Můstek

DIVADLO PONEC

Based in a building in the Žižkov district, just outside the New Town, Divadlo Ponec is a contemporary dance theater with an innovative schedule.

➕ J7 ✉ Husitská 24A ☎ 222 721 531 🚇 Florenc

DUPLEX

Overlooking the nocturnal animation of Wenceslas Square from its fifth-floor perch, this coolest of clubs is patronized by celebrities from all around.

➕ G8 ✉ Václavské náměstí 21 ☎ 732 221 111 🚇 Můstek or Muzeum

ROCK CZECH-STYLE

Before the Velvet Revolution in 1989, groups like the Plastic People of the Universe were seen as genuinely subversive of the existing order and were relentlessly hounded by State Security. Nowadays, the rock scene is a confused one, with a lot of fairly mindless imitation of western European trends but plenty of innovation, too.

HUDEBNÍ DIVADLO KARLÍN

Operettas and musicals are the undemanding fare in this suburban theater just beyond the inner city. Although badly damaged by the 2002 flood, the Karlín Music Theater is fully operational again, offering such spectacles as *The Addams Family* musical comedy hit from Broadway.

➕ J6 ✉ Křižíkova 10, Karlín ☎ 221 868 111 🚇 Florenc

LATERNA MAGIKA

The Magic Lantern's synthesis of film, music, theater and mime was developed in the 1950s by Alfréd Radok, and continues to intrigue and delight audiences. Some of the most successful shows are reworkings of ancient myths.

➕ F8 ✉ Nová scéna of the National Theater, Národní 4 ☎ 224 901 448 🚇 Národní třída

LUCERNA MUSIC BAR

This is part of the vast complex of the Lucerna Palace, a labyrinth of arcades and passageways that were the work of President Havel's builder-grandfather. Its good-sized ballroom can accommodate visiting groups as well as locals, and although some expats look down on it, it's the place to go for Czech retro.

➕ G8 ✉ Vodičkova 36 ☎ 224 217 108 🚇 Můstek

METROPOLITAN JAZZ CLUB

Swing, ragtime and blues abound at this well-established and popular jazz club.

🕂 G8 ✉ Jungmannova 14 ☎ 224 947 777 🚇 Národní třída or Můstek

NÁRODNÍ DIVADLO

The National Theater's magnificent auditorium is *the* place to soak up well-staged performances of such classics from the Czech operatic repertoire as *The Bartered Bride* or *The Cunning Little Vixen*. The schedule also features foreign operas, ballet and drama.

🕂 E8 ✉ Národní 2 ☎ 224 901 448 🚇 Národní třída

PALÁC AKROPOLIS

www.palacakropolis.com
The best club in Prague for live rock, house and world music is not in Nové Město but farther afield in the alternative and slightly edgy district of Žižkov.

🕂 Off map, J7 ✉ Kubelíkova 27 ☎ 296 330 911 🚇 Jiřího z Poděbrad

PALACE CINEMAS SLOVANSKÝ DŮM

In the Slovanský dům arcade running off Na příkopě, this is the most central of the Palace multiplexes, mostly showing a diet of subtitled blockbusters.

🕂 G7 ✉ Na příkopě 22 ☎ 255 742 021 🚇 Náměstí Republiky

RADOST FX

One of the most popular night spots in town, this club in a street behind the National Museum has been packing them in ever since it was established in the early 1990s.

🕂 H9 ✉ Bělehradská 120 ☎ 224 254 776 🚇 I P Pavlova

REDUTA

www.redutajazzclub.cz
Bill Clinton blew his sax at this best-known of Prague jazz locales during his presidential visit to Prague in 1994. Hear a variety of sounds, from Dixieland, swing and modern jazz.

🕂 F8 ✉ Národní 20 ☎ 224 933 487 🚇 Národní třída

ROCK CAFÉ

This downtown café and concert spot is the place to go if you like your rock music hard and very loud.

🕂 F8 ✉ Národní 20 ☎ 224 933 947 🚇 Národní třída

STÁTNÍ OPERA PRAHA (PRAGUE STATE OPERA)

Originally built in 1888 by Prague's German community as a rival to the exclusively Czech National Theater, the State Opera has a reputation for staging innovative productions of opera, ballet and drama.

🕂 H8 ✉ Wilsonova 4 ☎ 224 901 448 🚇 Muzeum

SVĚTOZOR

With a history going back to 1918, this is the most interesting art-house cinema in the city, with a pair of auditoriums screening subtitled foreign films, documentaries, animated films and much more.

🕂 G8 ✉ Vodičkova 41 ☎ 608 330 088 🚇 Můstek

VAGON

A popular rock venue that's heavy on heavy metal and revival acts, like the local talent Red Hot Chili Peppers Revival band.

🕂 F8 ✉ Národní 25 ☎ 733 737 301 🚇 Národní třída

VILA AMERIKA

This miniature baroque palace now houses a museum devoted to the renowned Czech composer Antonín Dvořák. Chamber concerts are held in its elegant salon, and during the season it makes a lovely setting for an evening show featuring some of Dvořák's best-known works.

🕂 G10 ✉ Ke Karlovu 20 ☎ 224 918 013 🚇 I P Pavlova

Restaurants

ALCRON (£££)

One of the city's most famous hotels offers fine dining in its La Rotonde restaurant, as well as unique taster menus in the intimate Alcron room, decorated with art deco murals.
🔲 G8 ✉ Štěpánská 40 (in the Radisson SAS Alcron) ☎ 222 820 000 🚇 Muzeum

CAFÉ LOUVRE (£)

A famous establishment now under its original name, the Louvre is decorated in rococo style and offers everything from breakfast to billiards. It also has a basement jazz club. The Louvre is requently voted café of the year by the *Prague Post* English-language newspaper.
🔲 F8 ✉ Národní 22 ☎ 224 930 949 🚇 Národní třída

FERDINANDA (£)

Just off Wenceslas Square, this friendly establishment dispenses fine beers from a country brewery as well as traditional Bohemian specialties.
🔲 H8 ✉ Opletalova 24 ☎ 222 244 302 🚇 Muzeum

GOVINDA VEGETARIAN RESTAURANT AND CLUB (£)

Plenty of whole food at this Hare Krishna restaurant/bakery/tearoom, in a convenient location not far from the art nouveau Obecní dům (Municipal House, ▷ 30).
🔲 H6 ✉ Soukenicka 27 ☎ 605 700 871 🕐 Mon–Fri 11–6, Sat 12–4 🚇 Náměstí Republiky

HOFFA (££)

This stylish modern bar mixes up great cocktails. It also offers a good range of local beers, wines and snacks, and weekly live music nights.
🔲 H7 ✉ Senovážne náměstí 22 ☎ 601 359 659 🚇 Staroměstská

HYBERNIA (£)

Two minutes on foot from the glamorous

Municipal House, this is a popular restaurant and wine cellar, known for generous portions of solid fare. Outdoor dining in season.
🔲 H7 ✉ Hybernská 7 ☎ 224 226 004 🚇 Náměstí Republiky

IMPERIAL (£–££)

This splendidly ornate early 20th-century café and restaurant, together with the adjoining hotel, has been immaculately restored to its former glory. Make the detour here, even if it's only for a coffee.
🔲 H6 ✉ Na poříčí 15 ☎ 246 011 600 🚇 Náměstí Republiky

KAVÁRNA EVROPA (£)

The art nouveau interior of the café attached to the famous Evropa Hotel is one of the sights of Prague, though service has not always matched the surroundings and at times an entrance fee has been charged.
🔲 G8 ✉ Václavské náměstí 25 ☎ 224 215 387 🚇 Můstek or Muzeum

NOVOMĚSTSKÝ PIVOVAR (£–££)

This brewery serves up its own light and dark lagers along with traditional Czech fare.
🔲 G8/9 ✉ Vodičkova 20 ☎ 222 231 662 🕐 Also open from 10am for breakfast Mon–Fri 🚋 Tram 3, 9, 14, 24 to Vodičkova

PIVOVARSKÝ DŮM (£–££)

The national beverage, beer, is given a creative spin at this microbrewery: try the coffee-flavored or sour cherry beers. Good food like roast pork and goulash. Often packed out, so book ahead.
🞣 G9 ✉ Ječná 15, at the corner of Lípová ☎ 296 216 666 🚇 I P Pavlova

PIZZERIA KMOTRA (£)

www.kmotra.cz/en/
As well as pizzas, pastas and risottos, seasonal local dishes are also served up here in a cavernous basement.
🞣 F8 ✉ V Jirchářích 12 ☎ 224 934 100 🚇 Můstek

POD KŘÍDLEM (££)

Stylish surroundings and impeccable Continental cuisine, with a selection of duck, pork and veal dishes. Also close to the National Theater.
🞣 F8 ✉ Národní 10 (entrance on Voršilská) ☎ 224 951 741 🚇 Národní třída

TRITON (££–£££)

The restaurant of the famous old Adria Hotel (▷ 112) is situated in its ancient cellars, which have been transformed into an atmospheric seabed grotto, complete with stalactite-encrusted ceiling. Attentive service and fine dining.
🞣 G8 ✉ Václayské náměstí 26 ☎ 221 081 218 🚇 Můstek

U BILE KRAVY (£££)

www.bilakrava.cz
French cuisine and steaks are the specialties of this small restaurant down a side street near the Národní muzeum (National Museum, ▷ 48). Very popular with locals too; book ahead on weekend evenings.
🞣 H9 ✉ Ruběsova 10 ☎ 224 235 970 🚇 Muzeum

U FLEKŮ (££)

A cavernous and many-roomed mock-Gothic beer hall with swarms of waiters and plenty of space for the tour groups who are its main customers. It's worth calling to sample the dark and tasty brew that's been made here for more than 500 years. Beyond the raucous interior, there's a beer garden.
🞣 F9 ✉ Křemencova 11 ☎ 224 934 019 🚇 Národní třída

U KALICHA (££)

Thanks to the Good Soldier Švejk's patronage in Austro-Hungarian days, this place is popular with visitors from abroad familiar with the famous

EXOTIC TASTES

The Lemon Leaf (£–££) is a good choice for Thai and international cuisine. It is a short walk from Karlovo náměstí. ✉ Na Zderaze 14 ☎ 224 919 056 🚇 Karlovo náměstí

Czech antihero. Solid food and accordion music is offered among much Švejkian memorabilia.
🞣 G10 ✉ Na Bojišti 12–14 ☎ 224 912 557 🚇 I P Pavlova

UNIVERSAL (£)

This restaurant is a cross between a French bistro and a Czech *hospoda* (pub), serving salads and pasta dishes, as well as traditional and international main courses.
🞣 F9 ✉ V Jirchářích 6 ☎ 224 934 416 🚇 Národní třída

U PINKASŮ (£–££)

This three-story pub with five dining halls was the first place in Prague to serve real Pilsner (in 1843). Enjoy refined dining upstairs in what is one of the best places to enjoy sustaining Bohemian specialties such as roast duck.
🞣 G8 ✉ Jungmannovo náměstí 16 ☎ 221 111 152 🚇 Můstek

U ŠUTERŮ (££)

A cozy place specializing in Czech treats like roast duck and fruit dumplings.
🞣 G8 ✉ Palackého 4, Nové Město ☎ 224 948 235 🚇 Můstek

VELRYBA (£)

Popular student café with a relaxed intellectual vibe, good coffee and light meals.
🞣 F9 ✉ Opatovická 24 ☎ 224 931 444 🚇 Národní třída

Hradčany

Hradčany takes its name from Prague Castle (Pražský hrad), the crag-topping citadel commanding the bridges of the River Vltava. The district extends along the hilltop to Strahovský klášter.

4

5

Na valech

Minist
Obrany

U Prašného

Mariánské hradby

P

Pražský
hrad

Jeleni

Královská
zahrada

HRADČANY

Oranžerie

Jiřský
klášter

Jizdárna
Praž hradu

Brusnice

6

Nový Svět

**Šternberský
palác**

Brusnice

**Bazilika a
klášter sv Jiří**

**Katedrála
sv Víta**

Nový Svět

sv Jan
Nepomucký

Martinický
palác

**Pražský
hrad**

Všech
svatých

Kanovnická

Starý
královský
palác

Keplerova

Kapucínská

Černinská

Brusnice

Loreta

**Arcibiskupský
palác**

U kasáren

Hradčanské
náměstí

Zám schody

**Černínský
palác**

Loretánské
náměstí

**Schwarzenberský
palác**

Ke Hradu

Nerudova

Hládkov

Keplerova

Loretánská

P

Úvoz

Parléřova

Pohořelec

**Lobkovická
zahrada**

Pohořelec

Dlabačov

7

**Strahovský
klášter**

Strahovská

**Strahovská
zahrada**

8

0 ——————— 250 m

0 ——————— 250 yds

B   **C**

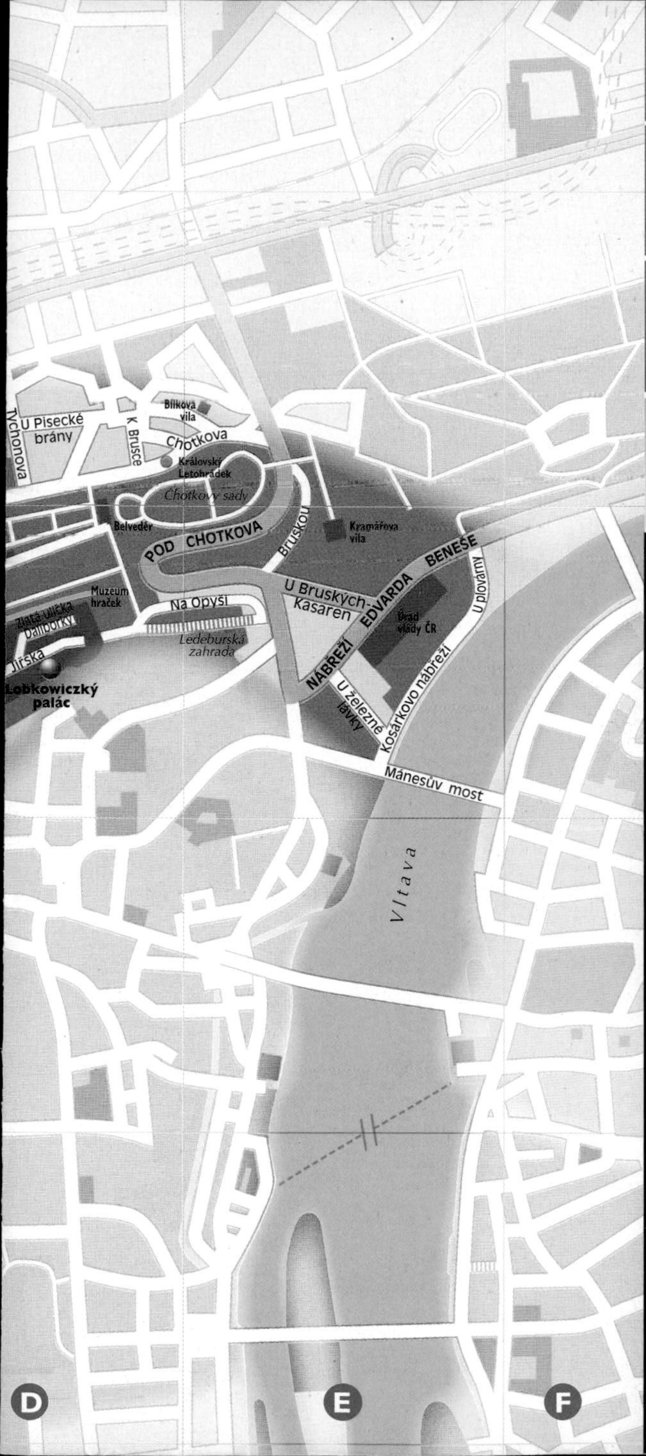

U Pisecké brány

Blíkova vila

Tvhonova

K Brusce

Chotkova

Královský Letohrádek

Chotkovy sady

Belvedér

POD CHOTKOVA

Brusnov

Kramářova vila

EDVARDA BENEŠE

Muzeum hraček

Zlatá ulička Daliborský

Na Opyši

U Bruských kasáren

Úřad vlády ČR

U plovárny

Jiřská

Ledeburská zahrada

NÁBŘEŽÍ

Kosárkovo nábřeží

Lobkowiczký palác

U železné lávky

Mánesův most

V l t a v a

D

E

F

Interior and exterior views of the Basilica of St. George

Bazilika a klášter sv Jiří

A blood-red baroque facade conceals the ancient interior of the Romanesque Basilica of St. George. Part of the Prague Castle complex, the basilica is now the setting for the National Gallery's collection of Czech art of the 19th century.

Bare basilica Founded in around 920, the basilica is the biggest church from this period in the Czech provinces and its twin towers and pale, sober interior stonework are a reminder of the great antiquity of the Prague Castle complex. Very well preserved, it is now a concert venue. The austere interior, a great hall with wooden ceiling, houses a small but impressive collection of artworks.

Paintings and princesses St. George's Convent was where young noblewomen were sent for the best possible education. Shut down in 1782 by Emperor Joseph, like many religious houses, it now houses the National Gallery's collection of Czech art of the 19th century. The nation seems to have produced more than its fair share of landscape painters, turning out conventionally Romantic evocations of Bohemia's woods, fields and mountains. Perhaps more interesting are the splendid canvases depicting dramatic moments in Czech history and mythology, while fine furniture and other objects drawn from the collections of the Uměleckoprůmyslové muzeum (Decorative Arts Museum, ▷ 34) show the development of arts and crafts.

THE BASICS

www.hrad.cz
➕ D6
✉ Jiřské náměstí
☎ Gallery: 257 531 644
🕐 Apr–Oct daily 9–5; Nov–Mar 9–4
🍴 Restaurants and cafés in castle
🚇 Malostranská, then an uphill walk
🚊 Tram 22 to Pražský hrad (Prague Castle)
♿ Few
✋ Expensive (included in general castle admission).

HIGHLIGHTS

Basilica
● Tomb of Prince Vratislav I
● St. Ludmila's chapel
● Renaissance south portal
Gallery
● L. Kohl: St Vitus Cathedral as it might have been
● J. Schikaneder: townscapes
● J. V. Myslbek: model of Wenceslas statue
● *Oldrich and Bozena*
● *The Egg Market in Prague*

Katedrála sv Víta

HIGHLIGHTS

● South Portal, with 14th-century mosaic
● St. Wenceslas's Chapel
● Crypt, with royal tombs
● Silver tomb of St. John Nepomuk
● West front sculptures

TIP

● You can get some idea of the glories of the cathedral by standing at the western end of the nave. To see its greatest treasures, like St. Wenceslas's Chapel, you will need to buy a general castle admission ticket.

To emerge into Prague Castle's Third Courtyard and see the twin towers of St. Vitus's Cathedral lancing skyward is truly breathtaking. The sight is all the more compelling when you realize that this Gothic edifice was completed within living memory.

Spanning the centuries The cathedral was begun by Emperor Charles IV in the mid-14th century. It is built over the foundations of much earlier predecessors: a round church erected by "Good King" (actually Prince) Wenceslas in the early 10th century and a big Romanesque building resembling the present-day Bazilika sv Jiří (▷ 67). The glory of the architecture is largely due to the Swabian builder Petr Parléř and his sons, who worked on the building for 60 years.

Clockwise from far left: Detail of the Alfons Mucha art nouveau stained-glass window; the silver tomb of St. John Nepomuk; the spires of the cathedral dominate the rooftops of the Hradčany; the arched ceiling of the Chapel of the Holy Cross; exterior; bronze chandelier (1532) in the gilded Chapel of St. Wenceslas

Progress was halted by the troubles of the 15th century, and the cathedral consisted only of an east end until the formation of an "Association for the Completion of the Cathedral", in 1843. Decades of effort saw the nave, western towers and much else brought to a triumphant conclusion; in 1929, a thousand years after Prince Wenceslas was assassinated, the cathedral was consecrated, dedicated to St. Vitus, commonly regarded as a patron saint of Bohemia.

Cathedral treasures The cathedral is a treasure house of Bohemian history, though the Crown Jewels, its greatest prize, are seldom on display. The spacious interior absorbs the crowds with ease and provides a fitting context for an array of precious objects that range from medieval paintings to modern stained glass.

THE BASICS

www.hrad.cz

✚ D6

✉ Pražský hrad

☎ 224 372 423

🕓 Apr–Oct daily 9–5; Nov–Mar 9–4. Tower: Apr–Oct daily 10–6; Nov–Mar 10–5

🍴 Restaurants and cafés in castle

🚋 Tram 22 to Pražský hrad (Prague Castle)

♿ Fair

💰 Free to stand at west end of interior, otherwise expensive

Loreta

Church exterior (left); archway (middle); roof statue (below)

THE BASICS

www.loreta.cz
+ B6
✉ Loretánské náměstí
☎ 220 516 740
🕐 Apr–Oct daily 9–12.15, 1–5; Nov–Mar 9.30–12.15, 1–4
🚊 Tram 22 to Pohořelec
♿ Few
💷 Moderate

HIGHLIGHTS

● The main facade, with statuary and carillon
● The Santa Casa
● Interior of the Church of the Nativity
● Diamond monstrance in the Loreto Treasury
● Cloister painting of St. Starosta

A bearded lady, skeletons rattling their bones to the sound of chiming bells, severed breasts and a flying house are not part of a freak show, but instead are all features of the sumptuous Loreto Shrine, on Hradčany Hill.

Counter-Reformation imagery After the Battle of White Mountain in 1620 Protestant austerity, with its repudiation of images, was replaced by the idolatry of the cult of the Virgin Mary, dripping with sensuality and symbolism. Of all the flights of architectural fantasy that the Roman Catholic Counter-Reformation perpetrated on Prague, the Loreto is the most bizarre as well as the most beautiful. Its church and courtyard are host to a display of cults, miracles and mysteries.

Weird wonders The kernel of the complex is a Santa Casa, a facsimile of the Virgin Mary's holy home in Nazareth, which, so tradition maintains, was flown by angels from the Holy Land and deposited at Loreto in Italy. It is an ornate little Renaissance pavilion built in 1631 and later given an equally ornate baroque setting of courtyard, carillon tower and richly decorated church. Pilgrims once flocked here in huge numbers to marvel at the macabre: St. Agatha offering up her bloody bosom to the angels; the skeletons in their wax death masks; unhappy St. Starosta, whose father killed her in a fury after finding that she'd grown a beard to discourage a preferred suitor.

TOP 25

Šternberský palác

Who would guess that the little alley beside the Prague archbishop's palace would lead to one of the nation's great art collections? Housed in the grand Šternberg Palace, it dazzles visitors with its old masters.

Ambitious aristocrats After building the Trojský zámek (Troja Château ▷ 98–99) on the edge of Prague, Count Šternberg, one of the city's richest men, needed a town house closer to Prague Castle. The Italian architect Giovanni Alliprandi designed the palace, and work began on the count's Hradčany home in 1698. However, the money ran out before the completion of the main facade. The interior was decorated with fine ceiling and wall paintings. It was a later Šternberg who donated much of the family's great picture collection to the precursor to the National Gallery in the early 19th century, and the nation's finest foreign paintings were housed here from 1821 to 1871. They are once more in this grand setting.

Picture palace Although tucked away behind Hradčanské náměstí, the Šternberg Palace is substantial, arranged around an imposing courtyard, with grand stairways and an oval pavilion facing the garden. The paintings of the National Gallery of European Art could keep an art lover busy for a day, though some star exhibits are no longer on view: The policy of restitution has returned them to the owners from whom they were confiscated by the Communists.

THE BASICS

www.ngprague.cz
🔁 C6
✉ Hradčanské náměstí 15
☎ 233 090 570
🕐 Tue–Sun 10–6
🍴 Café
🚊 Tram 22, 23 to Pražský hrad
♿ Few
💰 Moderate

HIGHLIGHTS

● Triptych of the *Adoration of the Magi*, Giertgen tot Sint Jans
● *Adam and Eve*, Cranach
● *Feast of the Rosary*, Dürer
● *Scholar in his Study*, Rembrandt
● *Head of Christ*, El Greco
● Portraits from 2nd-century Egypt
● *Beheading of St. Dorothy*, Hans Baldung Grien
● *Eleonora of Toledo*, Bronzino
● *St. Jerome*, Ribera

Pražský hrad

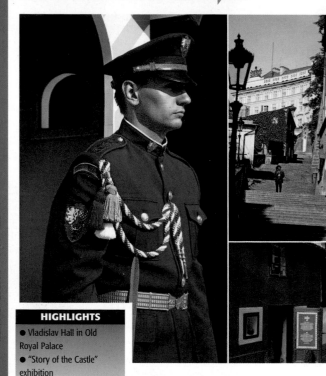

HIGHLIGHTS

● Vladislav Hall in Old
Royal Palace
● "Story of the Castle"
exhibition
● Golden Lane

TIPS

● The best time to see the
Changing of the Guard at
the western entrance is at
midday, when there is a
more elaborate ceremony,
enhanced by a musical
accompaniment.
● Combined entry tickets
offer a long or short tour
of the castle's attractions
(including the cathedral).
Check what you really want
to see before buying.

**The thousand windows of Prague Castle
gaze over the city. This is the citadel of
the Czech nation and it holds its
collective memory. It includes palaces,
churches, streets, squares and treasures.**

Castle denizens At the castle's western gates,
blue-uniformed guardsmen stand to attention beneath a pair of battling baroque giants.
Beyond, a series of courtyards echo with the
tread of countless ghosts: from emperors like
Charles IV and Rudolph II through to the rulers
of modern times.

Exploring the castle The castle offers plenty
of attractions. In the Starý královský palác (Old
Royal Palace), the gloriously vaulted Vladislavský
sál (Vladislav Hall) is spacious enough to have

Clockwise from far left: A guard in his box at Prague Castle; descending the Zámecké schody (New Castle Steps); detail of No. 13 Golden Lane (Zlatá ulička); the castle's Black Tower in the background; looking across the river toward Malá Strana and the castle; Golden Lane built into the fortifications of the castle

served for tournaments. In 1618, from an adjacent room, the Prague Defenestration took place, when Catholic councillors were thrown out into the moat, though a dungheap broke their fall. Their survival is marked by a monument in the gardens along the southern ramparts. The northern ramparts can be explored, too, and built into their walls are the brightly painted "alchemists' cottages" of Zlatá ulička (Golden Lane). To immerse yourself in the past of the castle, descend into its labyrinthine substructure, which now houses "The Story of the Castle", a succession of fascinating, state-of-the-art displays. Children will enjoy the Muzeum hraček (Toy Museum) just off Jiřská ulička, the lane leading down to the Černá věž (Black Tower) guarding the eastern entrance to the citadel.

THE BASICS

www.hrad.cz

✠ C/D6

✉ Pražský hrad

☎ 224 372 423

🕐 Courtyards and streets: daily until late. Buildings: Apr–Oct daily 9–5; Nov–Mar 9–4

🍴 Cafés and restaurants

Ⓜ Malostranská, then an uphill walk

🚋 Tram 22 to Pražský hrad

♿ Few

💲 Expensive

Strahovský klášter

HIGHLIGHTS

● 17th-century
Theological Hall
● 18th-century
Philosophical Hall
● Strahovská obrazárna
(Strahov Picture Gallery)
● 9th-century Strahov
Gospels

TIP

● Strahov has a Cabinet
of Curiosities in its lobby,
the weird and wonderful
objects here matched by the
microscopic oddities in the
Muzeum Miniatur on the far
side of the courtyard.

**Baroque spires rising to Heaven, a gilded
image of an enemy of the Faith, monks
profiting from an enterprise in Hell: The
Strahov Monastery seems to encapsulate
something of this paradoxical city.**

Persuasive priests The Strahov Monastery, a
landmark in the cityscape, crowns the steep
slope up from Malá Strana. It is a treasure-
house of literature, and its ornate library halls,
with their splendid frescoes, are among the
most magnificent in Europe. As befits a
monastery devoted to books, Strahov owed
much to its abbots' ways with words. Its 12th-
century founder, Abbot Zdík, persuaded Prince
Vladislav II to back his project by making flatter-
ing comparisons of Prague with the holy city of
Jerusalem. Much later, in 1783, Abbot Meyer

Detail of the ceiling fresco depicting the Banquet of King Balthasar, decorating the ceiling of the former abbot's dining room (left); the exterior of the monastery, with the statue of St. Norbert on the top (middle); the 9th-century Strahov Gospel, with a richly bejeweled cover, in the monastery (below)

exercised equal powers of persuasion on Emperor Joseph II to exempt Strahov from his edict that closed down many of the Habsburg Empire's monasteries. The cleric was so eloquent that Strahov benefited from the misfortune of other institutions: Books from the suppressed monastery at Louka were brought here by the wagonload. A gilded medallion of the emperor over the library entrance may also have helped to persuade Joseph that the Strahov monks deserved special treatment.

Returnees' revenge The monks, of the Premonstratensian Order, were chased out of Strahov by the Communists in 1952, but have come back. The upper floor of the cloisters is a gallery for the art returned to them; a wine cellar is now a restaurant called Peklo (Hell).

THE BASICS

www.strahovskyklaster.cz

B7

Strahovské nádvoří 1

233 107 711. Gallery: 233 107 746

Library halls: daily 9–12, 1–5. Gallery: Tue–Sun 9–12, 12.30–5

Peklo (Hell) restaurant in monastery cellars

Tram 22 to Pohořelec

Fair

Moderate

More to See

ARCIBISKUPSKÝ PALÁC (ARCHBISHOP'S PALACE)

The lusciously restored rococo facade fronts a truly sumptuous residence, unfortunately accessible only on special occasions.

➕ C6 ✉ Hradčanské náměstí 16 ☎ 220 392 111 🕒 Not normally open to public 🚌 Trams 22 to Pražský hrad

ČERNÍNSKÝ PALÁC (ČERNÍN PALACE)

This monstrous mass of masonry, one of the biggest of all Prague's palaces, was begun by Jan Humprecht, Count Czernin, in 1669, bankrupting his family for generations to come. Eventually it became a barracks, then the country's Foreign Ministry. In 1948, after the Communist coup, it was here that another infamous Prague defenestration took place, that of democratic Foreign Minister Jan Masaryk.

➕ B7 ✉ Loretánské náměstí 5 🕒 Not open to public 🚌 Tram 22, 23 to Pohořelec

KRÁLOVSKÁ ZAHRADA (ROYAL GARDENS)

The trees and lawns of the Royal Gardens stretch out along the plateau on the far side of the Stag Moat defending the northern flank of the Castle. Long ago they housed the imperial zoo, whose denizens included lions, tigers and even a dodo. Europe's first tulips were grown here. Nowadays the gardens offer an escape from the crowds, as well as providing unusual views of the castle and cathedral. At the eastern end of the garden stands the Belvedér. Also known as the Královský letohrádek (Royal Summer Palace), this lovely early Renaissance building, with its elegant arcade and roof in the shape of an upturned boat, was built in the mid-16th century by Ferdinand I for his beloved consort Queen Anna. At the center of the nearby formal garden, the Singing Fountain gets its name from the resonance made by the water falling into its basin.

➕ C/D6 ✉ Královská zahrada

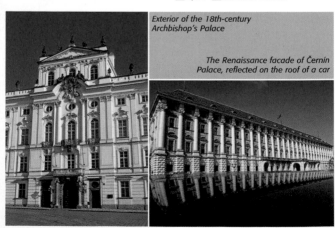

Exterior of the 18th-century Archbishop's Palace

The Renaissance facade of Černín Palace, reflected on the roof of a car

⏰ Apr, Oct daily 10–6; May, Sep 10–7; Jun, Jul 10–9; Aug 10–8 🚋 Tram 22 to Královský letohrádek or Pražský hrad 💲 Free

LOBKOWICZKÝ PALÁC (LOBKOWICZ PALACE)

One of Bohemia's great princely dynasties, the Lobkowicz family, has retaken possession of the Hradčany palace confiscated from them by the Communist regime. Inside are displayed treasures they accumulated over the centuries: arms and armor, porcelain, gold and silver, manuscript scores by the musicians they patronized such as Mozart and Beethoven, and above all wonderful paintings, among them townscapes by Canaletto and Pieter Brueghel's *Haymaking*.

➕ D6 ✉ Jiřská 3 ☎ 233 312 925 ⏰ Daily 10–6 💲 Expensive Ⓜ Malostranská

NOVÝ SVĚT

A world away from the pomp of Hradčany's palaces, this rustic little quarter is like a piece of countryside left over from the city's expansion. Basically consisting of a single winding lane, Nový Svět (New World) itself has become a quiet residential enclave and has resisted commercialization. In the past, its picturesque dwellings housed the castle's servants, as well as rather more eminent clients of the royal household such as astronomer Tycho Brahe and mathematician Johannes Kepler.

➕ B/C6 ✉ Nový Svět 🍴 U zlaté hrušky restaurant (▷ 80) at No. 3 🚋 Tram 22 to Brusnice ♿ Few

SCHWARZENBERSKÝ PALÁC (SCHWARZENBERG PALACE)

The city's most imposing Renaissance palace is just outside Prague Castle, its sgraffito-bedecked facade and bristling gables making a noble impression. It now houses the National Gallery's fine collection of baroque and mannerist art.

➕ C6 ✉ Hradčanské náměstí 2 ☎ 233 081 713 ⏰ Tue–Sun 10–6 🚋 Tram 22 to Pražský hrad 💲 Moderate

Exterior detail of the delightful Schwarzenberg Palace

Street sign and lamp on Nový Svět

Hradčany to Malá Strana

After exploring the byways of Hradčany, this walk follows an unusual route down to Malá Strana.

DISTANCE: 3km (2 miles) **ALLOW:** 1.5 hours

START

STRAHOVSKÝ KLÁŠTER
⊞ B7 🚋 Tram 22 to Pohořelec

END

MALOSTRANSKÉ NÁMĚSTÍ
⊞ D7 🚋 Tram 12, 20, 22

❶ At the courtyard of Strahovský klašter (▷ 74–75), turn right down steps that pass beneath the buildings.

❽ Turn right along Tomášská, which brings you into bustling Malostranské náměstí, with its busy tram stop.

❷ Turn right on emerging into the square, take the left fork and go left downhill to the Loreta (▷ 70). Bear left across the square and walk down the lane of Černínská.

❼ Turn right from either of the exits from the gardens into Valdštejnské náměstí (Wallenstein Square), dominated by the great palace (▷ 88) built by General Wallenstein, now the home of the Senate.

❸ This brings you to Nový Svět (▷ 77), where you turn right and walk along the winding cobbled street that brings you eventually into palace-lined Hradčanské náměstí.

❻ At the Moravská bašta, marked by a slim column, go down the steps and buy a ticket for the dramatic Palácové zahrady (Palace Gardens, ▷ 90), a series of terraces clinging to the precipitous slope.

❹ Enter the castle at the western entrance and walk to the Third Courtyard on the southern side of the cathedral. At the far end of the courtyard descend the stairway, to emerge into the gardens in the southern ramparts.

❺ Turn left and walk along the ramparts, enjoying the view down into Malá Strana.

HRADČANY WALK

Shopping

HŘAČKY

Tiny old-fashioned toy store loaded with traditional wooden toys, including spinning tops, cars, dragons and animals. Also hand-painted dolls, cloth dolls, games, and metal cars all at very reasonable prices. 🞧 B7 ✉ Lidická 11 ☎ 733 510 742 🚊 Tram 18, 22 to Keplerova, then a 3-min walk to Pohořelec

MUSEUM SHOP

This is probably the most tasteful and exclusive souvenir shop in Prague. Many of the items on sale have been inspired by artifacts in the rich collections on display on the upper floors of the palace, one of the city residences of the aristocratic Lobkowicz family. There are also books, as well as wines from the family's famous vineyards. 🞧 D6 ✉ Jiřská 3 ☎ 233 312 939 🚇 Malostranská

SHEVCHUK ART GALLERY

www.analogue.cz/ Ukrainian artist Yuri Shevchuk's cheery gallery sells a wide variety of his modern paintings, from portraits to colorful Prague cityscapes.

🞧 B7 ✉ Pohořelec 5 ☎ 776 140 519 🚊 Tram 22 to Keplerova

ŠIROKÝ DVŮR

Belying its cramped interior, this store offers a fantastic range of CDs, with expert and friendly assistance to guide you in your choice. As well as all the classical favorites, the vibrant Prague jazz scene is well represented and the proprietor will guide you through the riches of Bohemian and Moravian folk music. 🞧 B7 ✉ Loretánské náměstí 4 ☎ 220 515 403 🚊 Tram 22 to Pohořelec

HRADČANY SHOPPING

Restaurants

PRICES

Prices are approximate, based on a 3-course meal for one person.

£££ over 800Kč
££ 400Kč–800Kč
£ under 400Kč

HOTEL QUESTENBERK (££)

www.questenberk.cz
The restaurant of this small hotel just below Strahov Monastery offers more than adequate food as well as a fine outlook over Hradčany, Malá Strana, and the greenery of Petřín Hill.

🞡 B7 ✉ Úvoz 15 ☎ 220 407 600 🚊 Tram 22 to Pohořelec

LOBKOWICZ PALACE CAFÉ (£)

www.lobkowicz.cz
Occupying a couple of tastefully decorated rooms in a private palace forming part of the castle complex, this is easily the best place hereabouts for a snack or light meal, especially if you sit out on the balcony overlooking the castle gardens.

🞡 D6 ✉ Jiřská 3, Pražský hrad ☎ 233 356 978 🚇 Malostranská 🚊 Tram 22 to Pražský hrad

LVÍ DVŮR (££)

www.lvidvur.cz
In a strategic setting on the northern approach to the castle, the historic "Lion Court" serves meat such as venison, though the specialty is a whole suckling pig cooked on a spit.

🞡 C6 ✉ U Pražného mostu 6 ☎ 224 372 361 🚊 Tram 22 to Pražský hrad

TERASA U ZLATÉ STUDNĚ (££–£££)

www.terasauzlatestudne.cz
Pressed up against the southern ramparts of the castle, the restored "Golden Well" is one of Prague's most prestigious hotels and restaurants. Strictly speaking it is part of Malá Strana, but is included here for its lovely outdoor café reached by going down a few steps from the castle's south gardens.

🞡 D6 ✉ U Zlaté studně 166 ☎ 257 533 322 🚊 Tram 22 to Pražský hrad

U CÍSAŘŮ (££)

www.ucisaru.cz
This ancient building has an ambience worthy of its name, which means "At the Emperor's". The atmospheric, vaulted

BEWARE

Although Prague waiters have largely overcome a reputation for overcharging, it makes sense to check your bill carefully before paying for your meal. If service is not included in the bill and has been satisfactory, add 10 percent. Otherwise it is customary to make the total up to the nearest round figure.

rooms include arms and armor, aristocratic portraits, and the occasional bearskin. The menu is international and Czech cuisine.

🞡 C7 ✉ Loretánská 5 ☎ 220 518 484 🚊 Tram 22 to Pohořelec

U ZLATÉ HRUŠKY (£££)

www.restaurantuzlatehrusky.cz
Serving an interesting range of traditional Bohemian dishes as well as more international fare, the "Golden Pear" occupies a lovely old baroque residence on a charming lane. It also has an attractive garden section.

🞡 C7 ✉ Nový Svět 3 ☎ 220 941 244 🚊 Tram 22 to Brusnice

VILLA RICHTER RESTAURANTS (££–£££)

www.villarichter.cz
Once the preserve of the Communist elite, this dignified early 19th-century villa stands among the vines of the restored St. Wenceslas vineyard on the way up to the castle from Malostranská Metro. Diners can choose from a light snack at the more casual Terra restaurant, to a lavish meal at the grand Piano Nobile, all accompanied by some of the finest views over Prague.

🞡 E6 ✉ Staré zámecké schody 6 ☎ 702 205 108 🚇 Malostranská

Malá Strana

Perched below the castle, Malá Strana (Lesser Town) is Prague's most perfectly preserved historic district, an area of palaces and gardens, now peppered with chic restaurants and smart hotels.

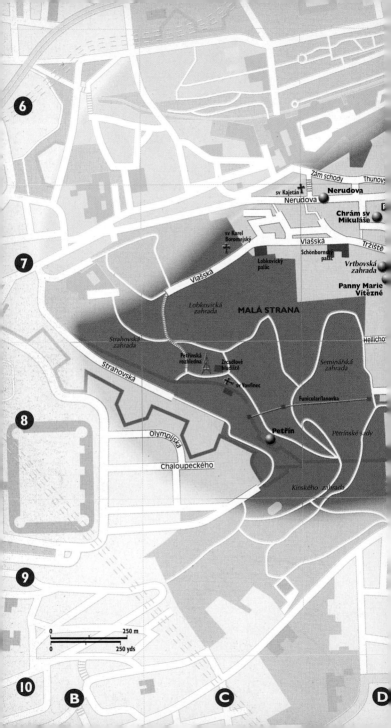

6

Zám schody   Thunovs

sv Kajetán **Nerudova**
Nerudova

**Chrám sv
Mikuláše**

sv Karel
Boromejský   Vlašská

Schönborns
palác

Lobkovický   **Vrtbovská
palác**   **zahrada**

7   Vlašská

Lobkovická   **MALÁ STRANA**   **Panny Marie
zahrada**   **Vítězné**

*Strahovská
zahrada*   Hellicho

*Petřínská   *Seminářská
rozhledna*   *Zrcadlové   zahrada*
Strahovská   bludiště*

sv Vavřinec

Funicular/lanovka

8   Olympijská

Petřín   *Petřínské sady*

Chaloupeckého

Kinského zahrada

9

0   250 m

0   250 yds

10

B   **C**   **D**

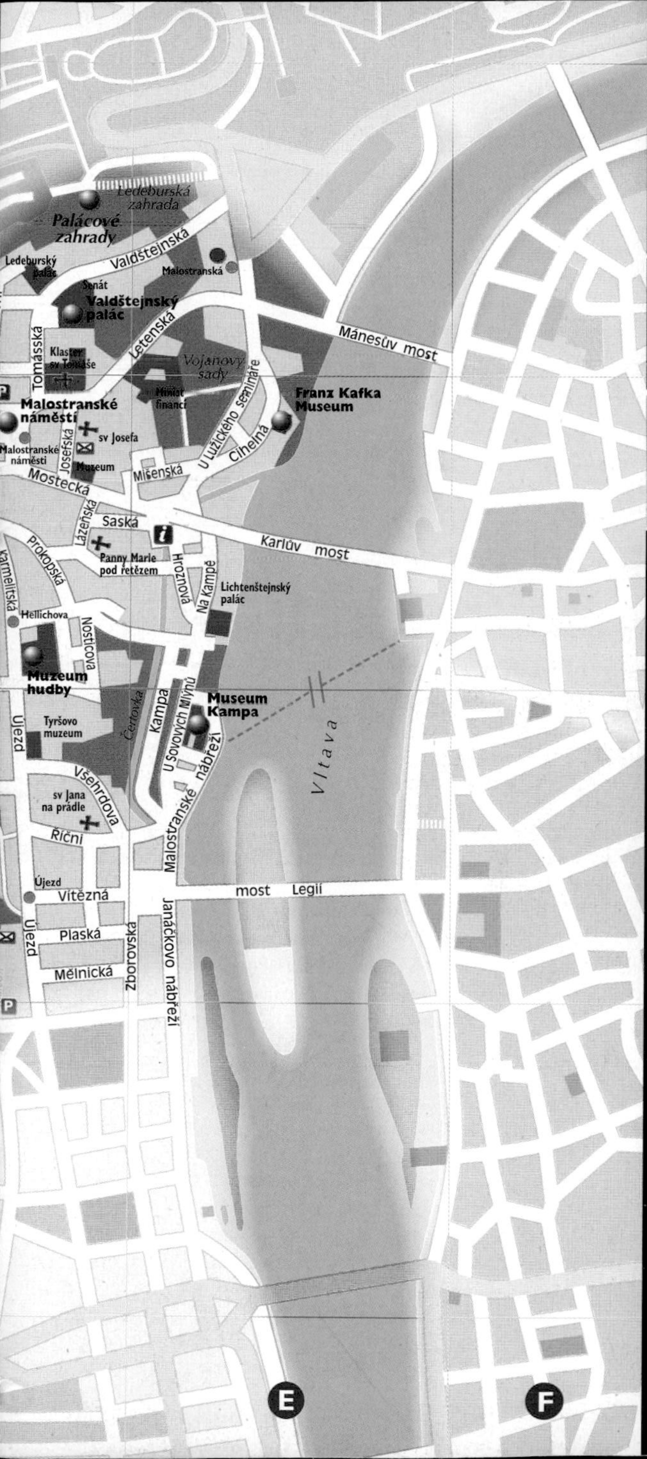

Ledeburská zahrada

Palácové zahrady

Ledeburský palác

Valdštejnská

Malostranská

Senát

Valdštejnský palác

Tomášská

Klášter sv. Tomáše

Letenská

Vojanovy sady

Malostranské náměstí

Minist. financí

Josefská

Franz Kafka Museum

sv. Josefa

U Lužického semináře

Cihelná

Malostranské náměstí

Museum

Mišenská

Mostecká

Lázeňská

Saská

i

Karlův most

Panny Marie pod řetězem

Prokopská

Karmelitská

Hellichova

Hroznová

Na Kampě

Lichtenštejnský palác

Nosticova

Muzeum hudby

Čertovka

Kampa

U Sovových Mlýnů

Museum Kampa

V l t a v a

Tyršovo muzeum

Všehrdova

sv. Jana na prádle

Újezd

Říční

Malostranské nábřeží

most Legii

Újezd

Vítězná

Zborovská

Plaská

Janáčkovo nábřeží

Mělnická

P

E   F

Malá Strana

Chrám sv Mikuláše

HIGHLIGHTS

● West front
● St. Barbara's Chapel
● Organ with fresco of
St. Cecilia
● Dome, decorated with
a magnificent fresco of the
Holy Trinity
● Huge sculptures of four
Church Fathers
● Trompe-l'oeil ceiling fresco
by Kracker

TIP

● The 215 steps of the
bell tower of St. Nicholas's
Church (entrance on south
side of the building) are well
worth climbing; from the
top there are fantastic views,
including close-ups of the
church's dome and statuary
as well as of the whole of
Malá Strana and the city
beyond.

**As you walk around the base of the lofty
St. Nicholas's Church, you feel the power
of the Catholic Counter-Reformation
expressed in one of the most beautiful
baroque buildings of Central Europe.**

Counter-Reformation citadel When the
Jesuits came to Prague following their rout
of the Protestant army at the Battle of White
Mountain, the existing 13th-century church
at the middle of Malostranské náměstí (Malá
Strana Square) was far too modest for their
aspirations. The new St. Nicholas's Church was
eventually completed in the 18th century and,
with its lofty walls and high dome and bell
tower, became one of the dominant features
of the city. The Jesuits intended their church
to impress, but not through size alone. They

Clockwise from far left: Frescoes decorating the walls and cupola; view from the church across the Vltava river to the towers of Týn Church, Powder Gate and St. Nicholas; looking across the silhouette of a statue at the church towers; the church organ played by Mozart; three statues sitting on the front of the church

employed the finest architects of the day (the Dientzenhofers, father and son, plus Anselmo Lurago), along with talented interior designers. Inside, no effort was spared to enthrall via the dynamic play of space, statuary and painting, a fantastically decorated pulpit and a 4,000-pipe organ (played by Mozart on several occasions). Today, the church still frequently holds classical music concerts.

Princely palaces and humbler households

In front of the huge church swirls the life of Malá Strana—locals waiting for the trams mixing with visitors following the Royal Way up to Hradčany. Malostranské náměstí is lined with a fascinating mixture of ancient town houses and grand palaces, while attached to St. Nicholas's is the Jesuits's college, now part of the university.

THE BASICS

www.stnicholas.cz

✚ D7

✉ Malostranské náměstí

☎ 257 534 215

🕐 Mar–Oct daily 9–5; Nov–Feb 9–4

🍴 Restaurants and cafés in square

🚇 Malostranská

🚌 Tram 12, 20, 22 to Malostranské náměstí

♿ Few

✋ Inexpensive; concerts expensive

Malostranské náměstí

Bar sign (left);
Lobkovický palác
(middle); aerial view
(right)

THE BASICS

➕ D7
✉ Malostranské náměstí
🚋 Tram 12, 20, 22 to
Malostranské náměstí

TIP

● The square offers
exciting possibilities for
taking photographs at all
times of day and night.
Floodlighting transforms the
great presence of the Church
of St. Nicholas, especially
when framed by the square's
arcades.

**Overlooked by the city's greatest
baroque church Chrám sv Mikuláše
(Church of St. Nicholas), Malá Strana
Square is the hub of the Lesser Town and
a focal point on the route between the
Old Town and the castle.**

A place to relax There's plenty to see and
explore in and around the square and nearby
streets and lanes. It's here in the heart of Malá
Strana (Lesser Town) that most visitors pause
before tackling the steep climb up to the
castle, not least because of the temptation
offered by the bars, cafés and restaurants.

The buildings St. Nicholas divides the sloping
square into an upper and a lower half, each
lined by the palaces and patrician houses so
characteristic of this part of town. Some are
very old, but most were rebuilt or given new
facades in baroque style in the late 17th and
18th centuries. The grandest of these is the
Lichtenštejnský palác (Lichtenstein Palace),
which takes up the whole of the western side
of the square. Built on the orders of Karl von
Lichtenstein (1569–1627), it now houses the
music faculty of the university, hosting recitals
and concerts. Take time to admire the broad
arcades of the burghers' houses along the
south of the square, and peer into the entrance
of No. 1/272, a fine example of an old-fashioned Prague *pavlač* (galleried courtyard);
it has the enchanting name of U petržílka
(Parsley House).

View to Vltava from the Petřín Tower (below); the Mirror Maze on the hill (right)

When the crowds on Charles Bridge become too much, there's always the glorious green of Petřín Hill—its orchards and woodlands a cool retreat from the city-center bustle and a real breath of the countryside in the metropolis.

A train with a view In 1891, for the city's great Jubilee Expo that celebrated the achievements of the Czech provinces when they still formed part of the Austrian Empire, the city leaders provided a jolly little funicular railway (the Lanovka) to the top of Petřín Hill. Now restored, it once again carries passengers effortlessly up the steep slope. At the top there's a whole array of attractions, including the Rozhledna (Lookout), the little brother of the Eiffel Tower, also built in 1891. Its 299 steps lead to a viewing platform, from where there is a wonderful panoramic view over the city. Next to the tower, the old-fashioned Mirror Maze (Bludiště) continues to work its hilarious magic. In the same building is an equally old-fashioned but effective diorama depicting an historic battle on Charles Bridge.

Country matters With its woods and orchards (splendid in spring), Petřín provides a welcome counterpoint to the busy castle area. Once there were vineyards on the hill, but these didn't survive the Thirty Years' War in the 17th century. They were replaced by the superb gardens that link the palaces of Malá Strana to the surrounding hillside parklands.

THE BASICS

➕ C/D 7–8
☎ 257 320 112
🕐 Rozhledna, Mirror Maze: Apr–Sep daily 10–10; Oct, Mar 10–8; Nov–Feb 10–6
🍽 Restaurant and café
🚋 Funicular railway, from Újezd in Malá Strana
🚊 Tram 22, 23 to Pohořelec, then walk
♿ Few
💰 Rozhledna, Mirror Maze: inexpensive

HIGHLIGHTS

● Rozhledna viewing tower
● 4th-century Hunger Wall
● Mirror Maze (Bludiště)
● Charles Bridge Battle diorama

Valdštejnský palác

Statues in the formal garden (left); relief work on a brass palace door (below)

THE BASICS

www.senat.cz

➕ D6

✉ Palace: Valdštejnské náměstí 17/4.
Garden: Letenská 10

☎ Palace and gardens: 257 071 111, 257 075 707

🕐 Palace: Jun–Sep Sat, Sun 10–6; Apr, May, Oct 10–5; Dec–Mar 10–4.
Garden: Jun–Sep Mon–Fri 7.30–7, Sat, Sun 10–7; Apr, May, Oct Mon–Fri 7.30–6, Sat, Sun 10–6

Ⓜ Malostranská

♿ Fair

✋ Free

HIGHLIGHTS

● Sala Terrena, with summer concerts
● Garden sculptures (copies of originals by de Vries)
● Grotesquery and aviary in garden

Think of Wallenstein Palace—Prague's biggest palace—as an awful reminder of the excessive ambition of its builder, Albrecht von Wallenstein, whose desire for power led to his assassination.

Greedy generalissimo Wallenstein's huge late Renaissance/early baroque palace crouches at the foot of Prague Castle as if waiting greedily to gobble it up. A whole city block was demolished to make way for the complex of five courtyards, a barracks, a riding school and a superb garden that were intended to reflect Wallenstein's wealth and status. Wallenstein (Valdštejn in Czech) turned the troubled early 17th century to his advantage. Having wormed his way into the emperor's good graces, he became governor of Prague, then Duke of Friedland. He married for money (twice), and great tracts of land (even towns) fell into his hands following the Battle of White Mountain in 1620 (panel, ▷ 124). His fortune grew more as he quartermastered the imperial armies as well as leading them. Rightly suspicious of his subject's intentions, the emperor had him killed.

Palace and garden The centerpiece of the palace, now the home of the Czech Senate, is the Great Hall with its extraordinary dynamic painting of Wallenstein as Mars, the God of War. The formal garden with its hedges, fountains and statuary is dominated by the superb Sala Terrena loggia, fashioned on those in Italy.

FRANZ KAFKA MUSEUM

www.kafkamuseum.cz

For all those who feel they should know more about the famous writer, this innovative exhibition holds the answer. The souvenir shop sells all of Kafka's works, as well as postcards, mugs, and much more besides.

➕ E7 ✉ Cihelná 2B ☎ 257 535 507 🕙 Daily 10–6 🚇 Malostranská 💴 Expensive

MUSEUM KAMPA

www.museumkampa.cz

This superb conversion of an historic mill houses an important collection of modern Czech art, with permanent as well as changing temporary exhibitions.

➕ E8 ✉ U Sovových mlýnů 2 ☎ 257 286 147 🕙 Daily 10–6 🚋 Trams 12, 20, 22, 23 to Hellichova 💴 Moderate/expensive

MUZEUM HUDBY

www.nm.cz

The National Museum of Music, in the stimulating setting of a Malá Strana church, exhibits instruments and memorabilia. After costly conversion, the nave now functions as a fine concert hall, overlooked by several floors of side galleries in which the collections are expertly displayed. Every conceivable type of instrument is on show, from violins once owned by virtuosos to some extremely odd-looking bagpipes—a Czech specialty. Even odder are the bulbous brass instruments arranged in artful patterns in their showcases.

➕ D7 ✉ Karmelitská 2/4 ☎ 257 257 777 🕙 Wed–Mon 10–6 🚋 Tram 12, 20, 22 to Hellichová 💴 Moderate

NERUDOVA

One of Prague's loveliest streets, Nerudova forms part of the Royal Route, rising steeply from Malá Strana Square toward the castle. The climb reveals many delights: baroque town houses with elaborate signs proclaiming their names ("The Three Little Fiddles", "The Golden Key"), and palaces with portals guarded by pairs of

Baroque and Renaissance buildings lining Nerudova

eagles or muscular moors. No. 47 ("The Two Suns") was the home of 19th-century writer Jan Neruda, who depicted the doings of the denizens of Malá Strana with a Dickensian pen.

➕ C/D7 ✉ Nerudova 201 🍴 Restaurants and cafés 🚋 Trams 12, 20, 22 to Malostranské náměstí ♿ Few

PALÁCOVÉ ZAHRADY (PALACE GARDENS)

This glorious group of terraced (formerly private) gardens of aristocratic families, clings to the near-vertical slope dropping from the castle ramparts to the palaces lining Valdštejnská street. Apart from their intrinsic attractiveness, they form an intriguing alternative route to and from the Hradčany heights (though only in season).

➕ D6 ✉ Valdštejnská náměstí 3 (also enter through Valdštejnská ul. 12) ☎ 733 557 571 🕐 Apr–Oct daily 10–6; May–Sep 10–7; Jun, Jul 10–9; Aug 10–8 🚇 Malostranská 🚋 Tram 12, 20, 22 to Malostranské náměstí 🎫 Moderate

PANNY MARIE VÍTĚZNÉ

www.pragjesu.info

Pilgrims from all over the world come to the Church of Our Lady of Victory to venerate the Bambino di Praga, a wax figurine of the infant Jesus given to the church in 1628. Originally dedicated to the Holy Trinity, the church was given its present name following the 1620 Battle of White Mountain, when it was handed over to the Spanish Carmelite order.

➕ D7 ✉ Karmelitská 9 ☎ 257 533 646 🕐 Church: Mon–Sat 8.30–7, Sun 8.30–8 (hours may vary). Museum: Mon–Sat 9.30–5.30, Sun 1–6 🚋 Tram 12, 20, 22 to Hellichova or Malostranské náměstí 🎫 Free

VRTBOVSKÁ ZAHRADA (VRTBA GARDEN)

www.vrtbovska.cz

Prague's finest individual baroque garden has sculptures and a view over Malá Strana.

➕ D7 ✉ Karmelitská 25 ☎ 272 088 350 🕐 Apr–Oct daily 10–7 🚋 Tram 12, 20, 22, 23 to Malostranské náměstí 🎫 Inexpensive

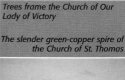

Trees frame the Church of Our Lady of Victory

The slender green-copper spire of the Church of St. Thomas

Malá Strana

This walk allows you to discover some of the less frequented parts of Prague's best-preserved historic district.

DISTANCE: 3.5km (2 miles) **ALLOW:** 2 hours

START

MALOSTRANSKÁ METRO
➕ E6 🚇 Malostranská

END

MALOSTRANSKÉ NÁMĚSTÍ
➕ D7 🚋 Tram 12, 20, 22

① From the station find your way to the upstream approach to Mánes Bridge. Turn right down steps into the little riverside park from where there are unusual Old Town views.

② At the far end of the park, turn left into Cihelná. The street is named after an old brickworks, now a restaurant. The Kafka Museum (▷ 89) is in its courtyard.

③ Walk in the same direction, bearing left over Čertovka (Devil's Brook), passing beneath one of the arches of the Charles Bridge (▷ 28–29).

④ You are now in Kampa Island. At the start of parkland go right to recross Čertovka. Bear right at the end of the park and follow a narrow street to Maltézské náměstí (Maltese Square).

⑧ Nerudova leads down into upper Malostranské náměstí (▷ 86). The busy tram stop is in the lower part of the square.

⑦ Go up little Šporkova opposite the German Embassy and follow it round, turning left up steps that bring you onto one of Prague's loveliest streets, Nerudova (▷ 89–90). Turn right and walk slowly downhill past baroque and rococo town houses.

⑥ Cross the road and walk up Tržiště. Continue uphill, bearing left into Vlašská. The magnificent Lobkowiczký palác (▷ 77) houses the German Embassy.

⑤ Walk across and head left into Prokopská at the far end, and turn right along busy Karmelitská.

Shopping

AHASVER ANTIQUES
An unusual little establishment, this antique shop sells an intriguing line in vintage apparel, lace, linen and accessories.
🔷 D7 ✉ Prokopská 3 ☎ 257 531 404 🚃 Tram 12, 20, 22 to Hellichova or Malostranské náměstí

KOŽEŠINY KUBÍN
A modest alternative to the grandiose Liska shop in the Old Town, this is a small, privately run fur and leather shop.
🔷 D8 ✉ Vítězná 12 ☎ 257 323 600 Ⓜ Újezd

LOUTKY MARIONETY
www.loutky.cz
Head here when not just any marionette will do, to find some of the finest handmade puppets available in Prague. The individual designs can be expensive but others are reasonably priced. Supplied by more than 30 different craftspeople.
🔷 D7 ✉ Nerudova 51 ☎ 774 418 236 🚃 Tram 12, 20, 22, 23 to Malostranské náměstí

PRAZSKY ALMANACH
www.artbook.cz
This antiquarian book store deals in art, history, poetry and rare out-of-

print editions. It also sells a selection of posters and postcards.
🔷 D8 ✉ Újezd 26 ☎ 224 812 247 🚃 Tram 20 to Újezd

VIA MUSICA
www.pragueticketoffice.com
Tucked into a corner of the Academy of Music in the Lichtenstein Palace (▷ 86), Via Musica stocks a wide selection of CDs and specializes in jazz and classical music. It is also a ticket office for concerts, theater, ballet and opera.
🔷 D7 ✉ Malostranské náměstí 13 ☎ 224 826 440 🚃 Tram 12, 20, 22 to Malostranské náměstí

Entertainment and Nightlife

JAZZ DOCK
www.jazzdock.cz
In a riverside location, Jazz Dock hosts some of the best jazz combos from the Czech Republic and further afield.
🔷 E9 ✉ Janačkovo nábřeží 2 ☎ 774 058 838 🚃 Tram 6, 9, 12, 20 to Arbesovo náměstí

MALOSTRANSKÉ BESEDA
This long-established club offers a varied program of jazz, blues and other sounds. There is also a café, restaurant and pub.

🔷 D7 ✉ Malostranské náměstí 21 ☎ 257 409

PRAGUE PUPPETS
Puppetry has a long tradition in the Czech lands, and puppets are certainly not just for children. Collectors pay good money for hand-carved marionettes, and there are several venues in the city that bring these dolls to life. Among the most-loved figures are those of the serio-comic duo of Speibl (father) and son Hurvínek.

123 🚃 Tram 12, 20, 22 to Malostranské náměstí

U MALĚHO GLENA
www.malyglen.cz
Little Glenn's is named after its genial owner, a devoted jazz fan whose club hosts live jazz and blues concerts nightly, featuring top artists from Prague and beyond. Sunday night jam sessions bring out some of Prague's best jazz musicians.
🔷 D7 ✉ Karmelitská 23 ☎ 257 531 717 🚃 Tram 12, 20, 22 to Malostranské náměstí

Restaurants

AQUARIUS (£££)

www.aquarius-prague.com
An elegant restaurant with a patio garden, where you can enjoy superb Mediterranean and Czech cuisine. The wine list is extensive.
🔒 D7 ✉ Tržiště 19 ☎ 257 286 019 🚋 Tram 20, 22 to Letenska

BAR BAR (£)

www.bar-bar.cz
Not a bar in the American or Western European sense, rather a relaxed student pub/café with good value sandwiches and salads. Large, but warm dining room. Friendly staff.
🔒 D8 ✉ Všehrdova 17 ☎ 257 312 246 🚇 Malostranská 🚋 Tram 6, 12, 20, 22 to Újezd

BARACNICKA RYCHTA (£)

www.baracnickarychta.cz
Tucked away down a back street, this local inn is great for tasty pub food, including *sauerkraut* and sweet dumplings (*ovocne knedliky*).
🔒 D7 ✉ Tržiště 23 ☎ 257 532 461 🚇 Malostranská 🚋 Tram 12 to Malostranské náměstí

BOHEMIA BAGEL (£)

A long-established hangout for North American expats and visitors, the Bohemia Bagel serves classic breakfasts, hearty soups and well-filled rolls, accompanied by an abundant supply of coffee.
🔒 D7 ✉ Lázenská 19 ☎ 257 218 192 🚋 Tram 12, 20, 22 to Malostranské náměstí

CAFÉ DE PARIS (££)

Excellent steaks and French-inspired cooking on one of Malá Strana's quietest and most romantic corners. The wine selection is one of the best in the local district, with plenty of affordable reds and whites—both Czech and French.
🔒 D7 ✉ Maltese náměstí 4 ☎ 603 160 718 🚇 Malostranská 🚋 Tram 12, 20, 22 to Malostranské náměstí

CAFÉ SAVOY (££)

Kafka hung out here when it was a humble café. Now more classy, it's gaining a reputation for its French-inspired cuisine and fresh seafood.
🔒 D8 ✉ Vítězná 5 ☎ 257 311 562 🚋 Tram 6, 9, 12, 20, 22 to Újezd

ČERNÝ OREL (£)

An enclosed courtyard and rustic interior lend this 18th-century inn the feeling of being removed from the bustling city streets and a place to chill out.
🔒 E7 ✉ U Lužického semináře 40 ☎ 257 531 738 🚇 Malostranská

CODA (£££)

www.codarestaurant.cz
Irresistible international dishes served in the stunning ambience of the covered courtyard of the Aria Hotel, or on a rooftop terrace in summer.
🔒 D7 ✉ Tržiště 9 ☎ 225 334 761 🚋 Tram 12, 20, 22 to Malostranské náměstí

EL CENTRO (££)

www.elcentro.cz
One of Prague's few authentic Spanish restaurants, with dishes from Andalucia and Latin America.
🔒 D7 ✉ Maltezske náměstí 9 ☎ 212 555 5500 🚋 Tram 5, 22 to Malostranské náměstí

GITANES (££)

This intimate little restaurant transports you

MALÁ STRANA RESTAURANTS

deep into the Balkans, with fiery food washed down with a selection of Mediterranean wines.

🕂 D7 ✉ Tržiště 7 ☎ 257 530 163 🚊 Tram 12, 20, 22 to Malostranské náměstí

HERGETOVA CIHELNA (£££)

www.kampagroup.com
Located in a converted brickworks, with an intriguing contemporary interior. The menu offers stylish, contemporary fare to match. Pleasant riverside terrace for warm summer evenings.

🕂 E7 ✉ Cihelná 2b ☎ 296 826 103 🚇 Malostranská

KAMPA PARK (£££)

www.kampagroup.com
The place to come for celebrity-spotting and the very finest cuisine in a lovely riverside setting.

🕂 E7 ✉ Na Kampě 8b ☎ 296 826 112 🚇 Malostranská 🚊 Tram 12, 22 to Malostranské náměstí

KOLKOVNA OLYMPIA (£)

www.kolkovna.cz/en
On the street leading to the Most legíí (Legions' Bridge), this is Prague's Left Bank equivalent of the Old Town's Kolkovna, one of the brewery super-pubs serving large por-tions of good Czech food accompanied by what many consider to be the best beer in the world.

🕂 D8 ✉ Vítěžná 7 ☎ 251 511 080 🚊 Tram 6, 9, 12, 20, 22 to Újezd

NEBOZÍZEK (££)

The first panoramic restaurant was opened on Petřín Hill more than 200 years ago, and the place is still a favorite with connoisseurs of romantic views and good food.

🕂 C8 ✉ Petřínské sady 411 ☎ 257 315 329 🚊 Tram 12, 20, 22 to Hellichova, then walk or take funicular uphill one stop

PÁLFFY PALÁC (£££)

www.palffy.cz
Offering first-rate cuisine in an unforgettable 18th-century palatial setting, this place has been popular for those in the know for years.

🕂 D6 ✉ Valdštejnská 14 ☎ 257 530 522 🚇 Malostranská

PETŘINSKÉ TERASY (££)

www.petrinsketerasy.cz
Enjoy well-prepared

Czech specialties on the terrace or in the winter garden, complemented by great views.

🕂 C8 ✉ Seminářská zahrada 13 ☎ 257 320 802 🚊 Tram 12, 20, 22 to Hellichova, then walk or take funicular uphill one stop

SOVOVY MLÝNY (££)

The restaurant attached to the modern art gallery in the beautifully restored "Sova's Mill" offers inter-national cuisine as well as innovative interpretations of traditional Bohemian dishes such as rabbit and goose. Riverside terrace.

🕂 E8 ✉ U Sovových Mlýnů, Kampa Island ☎ 257 535 900 🚊 Tram 12, 20, 22 to Hellichova

TRI STOLETI (££)

www.tristoleti.cz
A short hop over Charles Bridge, this restaurant is immensely popular for its contemporary fusion cuisine as well as its stylish decor.

🕂 E7 ✉ Misenská 4 ☎ 257 217 940 🚇 Malostranská

U MODRÉ KACHNIČKY (££–£££)

www.umodrekachnicky.cz
In its cozy side-street location the "Blue Duckling" continues to serve delicious variations on venerable Czech game and duck dishes.

🕂 D7 ✉ Nebovidská 6 ☎ 257 320 308 🚊 Tram 12, 20, 22 to Hellichova

Prague's suburbs and outer districts have much to offer. As well as musical shrines to Mozart and Dvořak there are historic buildings like Trojský zámek. The young-at-heart will enjoy the zoo.

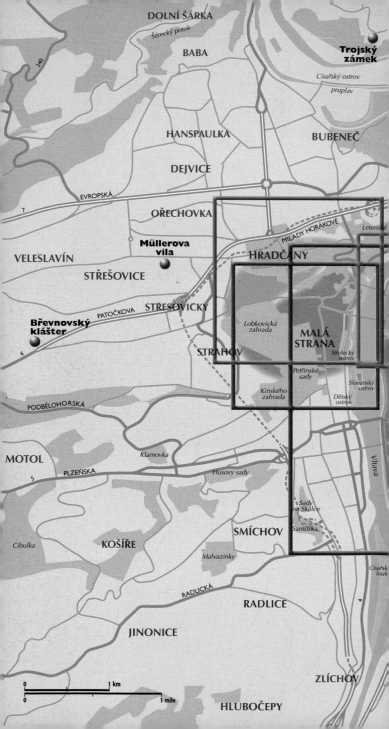

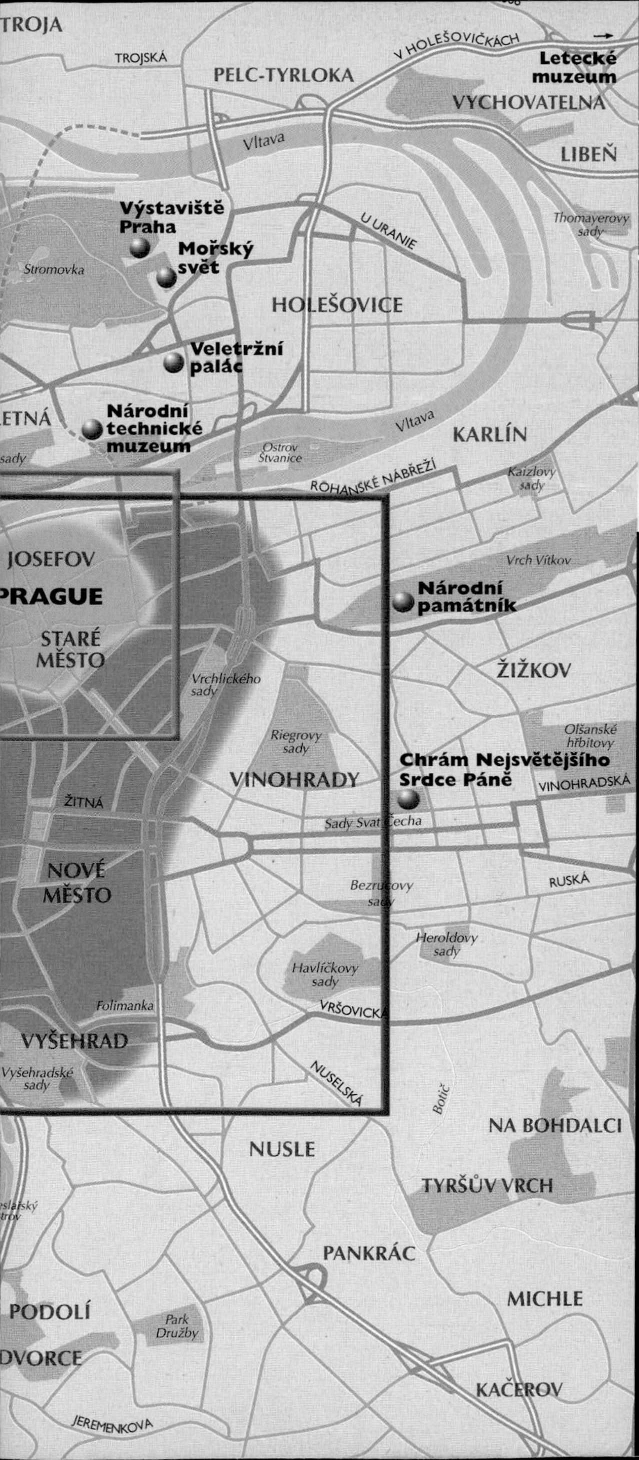

TROJA

TROJSKÁ

V HOLEŠOVIČKÁCH

PELC-TYRLOKA

Letecké muzeum

VYCHOVATELNA

LIBEŇ

Vltava

U URANIE

Výstaviště Praha

Mořský svět

Stromovka

Thomayerovy sady

HOLEŠOVICE

Veletržní palác

Národní technické muzeum

LETNÁ

sady

Vltava

KARLÍN

Ostrov Štvanice

ROHÁNSKÉ NÁBŘEŽÍ

Kaizlovy sady

JOSEFOV

Vrch Vítkov

PRAGUE

Národní památník

STARÉ MĚSTO

Vrchlického sady

ŽIŽKOV

Riegrovy sady

Olšanské hřbitovy

VINOHRADY

Chrám Nejsvětějšího Srdce Páně

VINOHRADSKÁ

ŽITNÁ

Sady Svat Čecha

NOVÉ MĚSTO

Bezručovy sady

RUSKÁ

Heroldovy sady

Havlíčkovy sady

Folimanka

VRŠOVICKÁ

VYŠEHRAD

Vyšehradské sady

NUSELSKÁ

Botič

NA BOHDALCI

NUSLE

TYRŠŮV VRCH

slavský břeh

PANKRÁC

MICHLE

PODOLÍ

Park Družby

DVORCE

KAČEROV

JEREMENKOVA

Trojský zámek

● Garden approach on river side of château
● South staircase and terrace with battling Titans
● Grand Hall paintings

TIP

● A good idea is to combine a trip to the Troja Château with a visit to the nearby Prague Zoo and Botanical Gardens (Botanika zahrada Praha, www.botanicka.cz).

Out here you catch a glimpse of how delightful Prague's countryside must have been three centuries ago, with vine-clad slopes, trees in abundance and the resplendent Troja Château among the allées and parterres.

Prague's Versailles This extravagant baroque palace was built not by the monarch, but by the second richest man in Prague, Count Wenceslas Adelbert Šternberg. The Šternbergs profited from the Thirty Years War, and at the end of the 17th century were in a position to commission Jean-Baptiste Mathey to design a country house along the lines of the contemporary châteaux of the architect's native France. The south-facing site by the river, orientated directly on St. Vitus's Cathedral and Prague Castle on the far side of

Clockwise from far left: The double staircase leading to the Troja Château; detail of an urn in the grounds of the château; the château's elegant red-and-white façade; formal parterres at the entrance to the château; wrought-iron gates at the entrance; the statue of a mermaid rising from the ornamental pond

the Royal Hunting Grounds, now Stromovka Park, was ideal for Šternberg, and it allowed him to offer the monarch the right kind of hospitality following a day's hunting.

Ornamental extravagance The palace's proportions are grandiose, and its painted interiors go over the top in paying homage to the country's Habsburg rulers. And over the top, too, goes a turbaned Turk as he topples, in stunning trompe l'oeil, from the mock battlements in the Grand Hall. The Troja Chateau was acquired by the state in the 1920s, but restored only in the late 1980s (some think somewhat excessively). It contains part of Prague's collection of 19th-century paintings, few of which can compete with the flamboyance of their setting.

THE BASICS

www.citygalleryprague.cz

✚ E1

✉ U Trojského zámku 1, Troja

☎ 283 851 614

🕐 Tue–Sun 10–6, Fri 1–6

🍽 Restaurant

🚇 Nádraží Holešovice, then bus 112 to Zoologická zahrada

🚊 Tram 5, 12, 14, 17 to Výstaviště, then walk across Stromovka Park and Císařský ostrov (Imperial Island) toward zoo

🚢 PPS boat from Palackého most, Nové Město

♿ Few

💳 Moderate

Veletržní palác

HIGHLIGHTS

- *Winter Evening in Town,* Jakub Schikaneder
- *Reader of Dostoyevsky,* Emil Filla
- *Serie C VI,* František Kupka
- *Melancholy,* Jan Zrzavý
- *Sailor,* Karel Dvořak

TIP

- Trying to see all the works on display in the Trade Fair Palace in one go is likely to lead to visual indigestion. Since tickets are available separately for the individual floors of the gallery, decide on your priorities and plan accordingly. If time is short, you might like to concentrate on the remarkable early-20th-century Czech painting and sculpture.

"A truly great experience was a tour of the Prague Trade Fair Building. The first impression…is breathtaking". So enthused architect Le Corbusier in 1928, shortly after this structure, now the Museum of Modern Art, was completed.

Trailblazer The great master builder and design pioneer Le Corbusier was vexed to find that his Czech colleagues had got in first in completing what is one of the key buildings in the evolution of 20th-century design, a secular, modern-day cathedral constructed in concrete, steel and glass. Set in the suburb of Holešovice, the palace was intended to be a showpiece for the products of Czechoslovakia. However, trade fairs moved away from Prague to Brno, and for many years the great building

Clockwise from top left: The exterior of Veletržní palác; galleries overlooking the building's central atrium; penny farthing bicycle with Contemplation (1893) by Jakub Schikaneder in background; Motorcyclist (Sunbeam), 1924, by Otakar Svec; 1960s Skoda convertible display; modern art on display in the museum's airy galleries

FARTHER AFIELD TOP 25

languished in neglect and obscurity, its originality forgotten as its architectural innovations became the norm throughout the world.

Disguised blessing After fire gutted the palace in 1974, it was decided to use its elegant spaces to display the National Gallery's modern art treasures, which had previously been without a proper home. The restoration took around 20 years. Now the engrossing Czech 19th-century collection leads the way to the amazing achievements of Czech artists in the early part of the 20th century; notably Alfons Mucha's Slav Epic series, a sequence of 20 immense canvases. The museum also shows works by French Impressionists and other modern foreign paintings, and promotes contemporary arts of all types.

THE BASICS

www.ngprague.cz
➕ H4
✉ Dukelských hrdinů 47, Holešovice
☎ 224 301 111
🕐 Tue–Sun 10–6
🍴 Café
🚇 Vltavská
🚋 Tram 12, 14, 17 to Veletržní
♿ Good
💰 Expensive

Národní technické muzeum

Fire engine (left); young visitors on a guided tour of the exhibits (right)

THE BASICS

www.ntm.cz

🚻 G5

✉ Kostelní 42, Holešovice

☎ 220 399 111

🕐 Tue–Fri 9–5.30, Sat–Sun 10–6

🚇 Vltavská then tram 25 to Letenské náměstí

🚋 Tram 15, 25, 26 to Letenské náměstí

♿ Few

💰 Expensive

HIGHLIGHTS

● 1928 Škoda fire engine
● Laurin and Klement soft-top roadster
● President Masaryk's V-12 Tatra
● Soviet ZIS 110B limousine
● Express locomotive 375-007 of 1911
● Imperial family's railway dining car of 1891
● Bleriot XI Kašpar monoplane
● Sokol monoplane

Did you know that Czechoslovakia had one of the world's biggest auto industries and that Škoda cars are legendary for their reliability? That a horse-drawn railway once linked Bohemia with Austria? That a Czechoslovak fleet once sailed the oceans?

Past glories The answer to all these questions will be "yes", after you've visited the National Technical Museum, off the beaten track on the edge of Letenské sady (Letná Plain). The museum celebrates the Czechs' long-standing technological prowess. The Czech provinces were the industrial powerhouse of the Austro-Hungarian Empire, and later, between the two world wars, independent Czechoslovakia's light industries led the world in innovation and quality.

Trains and boats and planes The museum's collection of technological objects is displayed to spectacular effect in the vast glass-roofed and galleried main hall, where balloons and biplanes hang in space above ranks of sinister-looking streamlined limousines and powerful steam engines. Deep underground there's a mock-up of a coal mine, and other sections tell you all you ever wanted to know about time, sound, geodesy, photography and technology. Since reopening in 2013 after extensive redevelopment, the museum's attractions include the Top Secret section, which reveals some intriguing espionage techno-tricks.

BŘEVNOSKÝ KLÁŠTER

www.brevnov.cz

The 1,000-year-old Benedictine monastery of Břevnov still has a rustic atmosphere. Its baroque buildings are the work of the Dientzenhofers, and include one of their grandest churches, and an array of other edifices.

➕ Off map A7 ✉ Markétská 1/28, Břevnov, Prague 6 ☎ 220 406 111 🕒 Apr–Oct Sat, Sun 10, 2, 4; Nov–Mar Sat, Sun 10, 2; guided tours only (in Czech) 🚊 Tram 22, 36 to Břevnovský klášter 💷 Inexpensive

CHRÁM NEJSVĚTĚJŠÍHO SRDCE PÁNĚ

Completed in 1932, the early modern Sacred Heart Church, in Vinohrady is the masterwork of the Slovene architect Josip Plečnik, noted for his transformation of Prague Castle in the interwar years.

➕ Off map J9 ✉ Náměstí Jiřího z Poděbrad 19, Vinohrady ☎ 222 727 713 🕒 40 min before and after services. Sun 9, 11 and 6; Mon–Sat 8 and 6 🚊 Tram 11 to Jiřího z Poděbrad

LETECKÉ MUZEUM

www.vhu.cz

This has one of Europe's largest collections of historic aircraft. Interwar machines demonstrate the energy of the Czechoslovak aircraft industry then. But the stars of the show are the World War II aircraft.

➕ Off map J1 ✉ Mladoboleslavská 902, Kbely ☎ 973 207 500 🕒 May–Oct Tue–Sun 10–6 🚊 Letňany, then bus 185, 259, 269, 302, 376 to Letecké Muzeum 💷 Free

MOŘSKÝ SVĚT

www.morsky-svet.cz

Within the Výstaviště Praha (▷ 104), the aquarium is the largest in the country, with fish and other aquatic species from all over the world. Highlights include sharks, piranhas and turtles, and there is a tank where visitors can feed the sea creatures.

➕ H3 ✉ Výstaviště, Holešovice ☎ 220 103 275 🕒 Daily 10–7 🚊 Nadrazi Holešovice 🚊 Tram 12, 17, 24 💷 Expensive, family ticket available

The striking structure of the Sacred Heart Church

The interior vaults of the Benedictine monastery of Břevnov

MÜLLEROVA VILA

www.mullerovavila.cz

The villa, built for the Müller family in 1930, is a key building in the evolution of Functionalist architecture. Its designer was the Viennese architect Adolf Loos (1870–1933). The exterior is severe, but the spatial austerity of the interior is relieved by the use of precious materials.

🔼 A6 ✉ Nad Hradním vodojemem 14, Střešovice, Prague 6 ☎ 224 312 012 🕒 Guided tours Apr–Oct Tue, Thu, Sat, Sun at 9, 11, 1, 3, 5; Nov–Mar 10, 12, 2, 4. Tours must be booked ahead 🚇 Hradčanská, then tram 🚊 Tram 1, 2, 18 to Ořechovka 💰 Expensive

NÁRODNÍ PAMÁTNÍK (NATIONAL MEMORIAL)

Built to commemorate the Czechoslovak legions that fought on the Allied side in World War I, this great slab of a building overlooking the city includes what is claimed to be the largest equestrian statue in the world: the 162-tonne colossus celebrates the Hussite general Jan Zizka, one of the great heroes of Czech history. The interior of the building has historical displays and is extravagantly decorated with Communist-era art. There's an extraordinary chapel with depictions of Soviet soldiers instead of saints, as well as a basement where embalmers once strove to preserve the mummified corpses of Party leaders. Climb to the rooftop for fantastic views over the city.

🔼 Off map J7 ✉ U Památníku 1900 ☎ 222 781 676 🕒 Apr–Oct Wed–Sun 10–6; Nov–Mar Thu–Sun 10–6 🚌 133, 175 to U Památníku and steep uphill walk 💰 Moderate

VÝSTAVIŠTĚ PRAHA

The art nouveau Exhibition Grounds offer an array of attractions, including amusement park, performance spaces, a lapidarium and a fine fountain. Nearby is the Planetarium.

🔼 G/H3 ✉ U Výstaviště, Holešovice ☎ 220 103 111 🕒 Daily, hours vary 🍴 Cafés and restaurants 🚊 Tram 5, 12, 14, 17 to Výstaviště 💰 Inexpensive

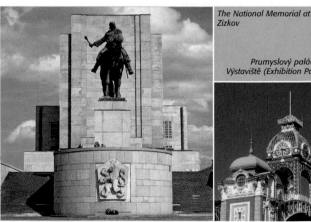

The National Memorial at Zizkov

Prumyslový palác in Výstaviště (Exhibition Park)

HRAD KARLŠTEJN (KARLŠTEJN CASTLE)

This mighty fortress, one of the great sights of Bohemia, towers above the glorious woodlands of the gorge of the River Berounka, 40 minutes' drive from Prague. The castle was started in 1348 by the Emperor Charles IV who conceived it as a sort of sacred bunker, a repository for the Crown Jewels and his collection of holy relics. Book tours in advance.

THE BASICS

www.hradkarlstejn.cz
Distance: 35km (21 miles)
Journey Time: 40 min
☎ Tours: 274 008 154; castle: 311 681 617
🚆 Prague–Smíchov to Karlštejn

ZÁMEK KONOPIŠTĚ (KONOPIŠTĚ CASTLE)

Konopiště Castle's round towers rise in romantic fashion above the surrounding woodlands. The palace's origins date to the 14th century, but it owes its present appearance largely to Archduke Franz Ferdinand, heir to the Habsburg throne, who filled it with fine furniture, a weapons collection and trophies of the countless wild creatures he slaughtered. The archduke met his own violent end when he was cut down by an assassin's bullet in Sarajevo, triggering the start of World War I.

THE BASICS

www.zamek-konopiste.cz
Distance: 43km (26 miles)
Journey Time: 45 min by car; 1 hour by train then short trip by local bus or taxi
☎ 317 721 336 🕐 Apr–May Tue–Sun 10–12, 1–4; Jun–Aug 10–12, 1–5; Sep 10–12, 1–4; Oct–Nov 10–12, 1–3 🚆 Hlavní nádraží to Benešov then bus or taxi

KUTNA HORA

One of Bohemia's best-preserved old towns has abundant relics from the glory days when it was a great silver mining hub. A stroll around the streets leads past many minor treasures, such as the Gothic Kamenný dům (Stone House) and the venerable 12-sided public fountain. The town's finest monument is the great Chrám svaté Barbory (St. Barbara's Church), a cathedral-size structure, one of Europe's most extraordinary achievements of late Gothic architecture. In the suburb of Sedlec is a macabre item, the bones from some 40,000 burials in a vaulted ossuary.

THE BASICS

www.kutnahora.cz
Distance: 70km (43 miles)
Journey Time: 1 hour 15 min by bus from Florenc bus station
ℹ Sankturinovský dům, Palackého náměstí, 284 01 Kutná Hora
☎ 327 511 259

THE BASICS

Distance: 27km (17 miles)
Journey time: 50 min by local train from Masarykovo nádraží

Zámek Nelahozeves
www.lobkowiczevents.cz
✉ 27751 Nelahozeves
🕒 Apr–Oct Tue–Sun 9–5 (guided tour only)

Památník Antonín Dvořáka
www.nm.cz
✉ 27751 Nelahozeves
🕒 Apr–Jun, Sep–Oct Tue–Sun 10–4; Jul–Aug 10–5 Jan–Mar, Nov–Dec 10–3

NELAHOZEVES

This otherwise unpretentious village on the banks of the Vltava north of Prague has two major attractions, Památník Antonín Dvořáka (the birthplace of composer Antonín Dvořák), and a magnificent château, Zámek Nelahozeves. Dvořák's humble home has plenty of memorabilia (tel: 315 785 099), while the castle, a splendid example of Italian-inspired Bohemian Renaissance architecture, is a treasure house (tel: 315 709 111 to book a tour). A permanent exhibition entitled "Private Space: a noble family at home", features 12 fully furnished period rooms. The building itself, approached via a bridge across a dry moat, has three completed wings on the courtyard, in different styles. Although the interior is now mostly visited for the collections, there are many fascinating areas, particularly the Arkádové haly (Arcade Hall) and the vaulted Rytířský sál (Knights Hall).

THE BASICS

www.pamatnik-terezin.cz
Distance: 65km (40 miles)
Journey time: Around 1 hour from Florenc bus station
ℹ️ Terezín–Památník (Terezín–Memorial), Principova alej 304, 411 55 Terezín
☎ 416 782 225
🕒 Museum: Apr–Oct daily 10–6; Nov–Mar 10–4

TEREZIN

In World War II, the Nazis cleared this 18th-century barrack town of its inhabitants and turned it into a ghetto for Czechoslovak and German Jews. Deceitfully portraying it as a model community, they succeeded in fooling the International Red Cross, but in reality Terezín was simply a staging post for the Final Solution, and most of those incarcerated here met their end in Auschwitz. The Muzeum Ghetta (Ghetto Museum) tells the awful story. Outside the walls is the Malá pevnost (Small Fortress). Originally an Austrian political prison, it became a far more horrible jail for Gestapo victims of many nationalities and finally, in 1945, an appallingly run holding camp for German expellees.

Like all major cities, Prague has a range of accommodations, from sleek, modern hotels and magnificent converted old buildings to hostels and cottages.

Where to Stay

Introduction

Prague offers an extraordinary range of places to stay in almost every category, with a distinct emphasis on hotels in historic buildings.

New Hotels

A building boom has created an impressive increase in the number of four- and five-star establishments in Prague. While official room rates remain high in the city, there are many special offers available and bargaining can sometimes yield substantial reductions. Prague is an all-seasons city, and it is prudent to make reservations well in advance, no matter what time of the year you intend to travel.

Practical Considerations

The location of your accommodations is crucial. Efficient public transport may get you quickly from your suburban hotel to the city, but since Prague is such a delight to explore on foot, you may want to look for lodgings in one of the historic quarters within walking distance of some of the city's principal attractions. Room rates are usually quoted in euros rather than Czech crowns. Credit cards are widely accepted.

Longer Stays

If you intend staying more than a few days, it could well be worthwhile renting an apartment or even a room in a private flat. Some of the former are in outstanding settings, with, for example, river views, while private rooms tend to be out in the suburbs.

ACCOMMODATIONS ADVICE

If you are arriving in the city without a hotel reservation, one of the most reliable kiosks at Prague airport is that of the Prague Information Service (P.I.S), who also can arrange accommodations at its other information offices, as well as online (www.praguewelcome.cz/en/stay). An excellent private apartment service is "Apartments in Prague" ☎ 777 761 738; from UK 020 8144 3332; www.apartmentsinprague.co.uk

You can stay in grand old buildings when you visit Prague

Budget Hotels

PRICES

Expect to pay up to 2,750Kč (€98) per night for a budget hotel.

ANNA

www.hotelanna.cz
A reliable 26-room hotel in the pleasant inner suburb of Vinohrady, less than 15 minutes' stroll from Wenceslas Square.
Off map J10 ⊠ Budečská 17, Vinohrady ☎ 222 513 111 ⊗ Náměstí Míru

ATLANTIC

www.hotel-atlantic.cz
Just around the corner from the Municipal House, this medium-size place is a member of the Small Charming Hotels group.
H6 ⊠ Na Poříčí 9, eastern New Town ☎ 224 811 084 ⊗ Náměstí Republiky

BÍLÝ LEV

www.hotelbilylev.cz
A good-value, 27-room place in the emerging eastern suburb of Žižkov.
Off map J7 ⊠ Cimburkova 20 ☎ 222 780 430 ⊗ Trams 5, 9, 26 to Husinecká

HAŠTAL

www.hastal.com
A comfortable 24-room hotel, in a former brewery with splendid views over a quiet square.
G6 ⊠ Haštalská 16, Staré Město ☎ 222 314 335 ⊗ Tram 5, 14, 26 to Dlouhá třída

HOTEL ARBES

www.hotelarbes.cz
A family-run hotel located midway between Malá Strana and the Anděl shopping area. Request a quieter room overlooking the courtyard.
D9 ⊠ Viktora Huga 3, Smíchov ☎ 251 116 555 ⊗ Anděl

HOTEL WILLIAM

www.hotelwilliam.cz
Near Charles Bridge, this friendly hotel has 43 spacious, modern rooms and a good buffet breakfast. It's on the tram route, so ask for one of the quieter rooms at the back of the building.
D7 ⊠ Helichova 5, Mala Strana ☎ 257 320 242 ⊗ Tram 12, 20 or 22 to Helichova

KAFKA

www.kafka.prague-hostels.cz
This excellent value, 50-room hotel in the suburb of Žižkov, is only

HOSTELS

A number of hostels stand ready to look after the swarms of backpackers passing through Prague on their travels. A popular one offering single rooms as well as dorms and with several branches in the city and elsewhere is:
Traveller's Hostel
www.travellers.cz
G6 ⊠ Dlouhá 33, Old Town ☎ 224 826 662 ⊗ Náměstí Republiky

10 minutes' walk from the main train station.
G4 ⊠ Cimburkova 24 ☎ 222 333 116 ⊗ Tram 5, 9, 26 to Husinecká

NOVOMĚSTSKÝ HOTEL

www.novomestskyhotel.cz
A small hotel on a quiet street by the New Town Hall, with a high standard for the lowish room rates.
G9 ⊠ Řeznická 4, Nové Město ☎ 221 419 911 ⊗ Karlovo náměstí

SALVATOR

www.salvator.cz
Friendly, 32-room courtyard hotel, very near the Municipal House. Also has upscale apartments in nearby building.
H6 ⊠ Truhlářská 10, Nové Město ☎ 222 312 234 ⊗ Náměstí Republiky

TARA

www.pensiontara.net
A straightforward, eight-room pension in the heart of the Old Town. Note there is no elevator to rooms on the second, third and fourth floors.
F7 ⊠ Havelská 15, Staré Město ☎ 224 228 083 ⊗ Můstek

U LILIE

www.pensionulilie.cz
This 17-room pension, with plain, quiet rooms, is in a medieval house close to Charles Bridge. Restaurant and free WiFi.
F7 ⊠ Liliová 15, Staré Město ☎ 222 220 432 ⊗ Staroměstská

109

Mid-Range Hotels

WHERE TO STAY MID-RANGE HOTELS

AMETYST
www.hotelametyst.cz
A fresh and inviting 84-room, family-owned hotel, with wine bar and sauna, and only a 10-minute walk from Wenceslas Square.
J10 Jana Masaryka 11, Vinohrady 222 921 946
Náměstí Míru

BEST WESTERN METEOR PLAZA
www.hotel-meteor.cz
Almost opposite the Powder Tower and Municipal House, this modern hotel with a full range of facilities looks back on a long history of offering hospitality to the great and good.
H7 Hybernská 6
224 192 111 Náměstí Republiky

BETLEM CLUB
www.betlemclub.cz
A small 21-room hotel offering accommodations in the same square as Jan Hus's historic Bethlehem Chapel in the heart of the Old Town.
F8 Betlémské náměstí 9, Staré Město 222 221 574 Národní třída

CENTRAL
www.central-hotel-prague.com
With refurbished, well equipped rooms, the Central is located behind the Municipal House, with 68 rooms.
G7 Rybná 8, Staré Město 224 812 041
Náměstí Republiky

CLOISTER INN
www.cloister-inn.com
A bright, cheery modern hotel with 73 rooms built on the site of the 17th-century Convent of St Bartholomew between the National Theater and the Bethlehem Chapel.
F8 Konviktská 14, Staré Město 224 211 020
Národní třída

HOTEL 16
www.hotel16.cz
Excellent-value family hotel, with 14 rooms. Close to the Dvořák Museum and the botanical gardens, and 15-minutes' walk from Wenceslas Square.
G10 Kateřinská 16, Nové Město 224 920 636
I P Pavlova

BOTELS

An alternative to conventional hotels are the "botels" moored at various points along the banks of the Vltava. However, being rather cramped, they are less romantic than they might sound. Close to the Palacký Bridge (Palackého most) on the Smíchov quayside, try the Admirál (257 321 302; www.admiral-botel.cz).

IBIS
www.ibis.com/Prague
The Accor group has three hotels in Prague bearing the Ibis name, all of which offer reliable, accommodations and facilities. Of the three, the most centrally located is the Ibis Praha Old Town; the claimed location is a bit of an exaggeration since it is actually in the eastern part of the New Town, albeit literally just a few steps from the Municipal House.
H7 (Ibis Praha Old Town)
Na Poříčí 5, eastern New Town 266 000 999
Náměstí Republiky

INTERNATIONAL PRAGUE
www.internationalprague.com
This Stalinist skyscraper designed in typical grandiose wedding-cake style has been brought up-to-date, but still has something of the intriguing atmosphere of the Communist era.
Off map D5 Koulova 15 296 537 111 Tram 20 to Podbaba

LUNÍK
www.hotel-lunik.cz
Special offers can bring this comfortable, family-style small hotel into the affordable category. It's just a few steps from the nearest metro station and an easy walk to the top of Wenceslas Square.
H9 Londýnská 50, Vinohrady 224 253 974
Náměstí Míru

MAXIMILIAN

www.maximilianhotel.com
This 1904 building has been beautifully reconstructed in art nouveau style with attention to every detail. Top of the range, with beauty spa—try for one of their deals.
🚇 G6 ✉ Haštalská 14, Staré Město ☎ 225 303 118 🚊 Tram 5, 14 to Dlouhá třída

METAMORPHIS

www.metamorphis.cz
Few settings are as romantic as the medieval cobbled courtyard of the Ungelt (Týnský dvůr), and few hotels as atmospheric as this ancient edifice with its vaults and exposed beams.
🚇 G7 ✉ Malá Štupartská 5 ☎ 221 771 011 🚊 Náměstí Republiky

NH PRAGUE

www.nh-hotels.com
High standard of comfort and facilities in the Smíchov branch of this chain, whose buildings are spectacularly linked by funicular. With 436 rooms.
🚇 C11 ✉ Mozartova 1 ☎ 257 153 111 🚊 Anděl

SAX

www.sax.cz
This 22-room hotel just off Nerudova Street offers views of Malá Strana. Now stunningly fitted out in 1960s-style retro furnishings.
🚇 C7 ✉ Janský vršek 3 ☎ 257 531 268 🚊 Tram 12, 22, 23 to Malostranské náměstí, then an uphill walk

SIEBER

www.sieberhotel-prague.com
This gracious family-run hotel offers 20 luxurious rooms and suites. A step up from the average mid-range hotel.
🚇 Off map J9 ✉ Slezská 55, Vinohrady ☎ 608 503 728 🚊 Jiřího z Poděbrad 🚊 Tram 10, 16 to Perunova

TCHAIKOVSKY

A tasteful 19-room hotel near Karlovo náměstí, the Dvořák museum and the botanical gardens.
🚇 G10 ✉ Ke Karlovu 19, Nové Město ☎ 224 912 121 🚊 Karlovo náměstí or I P Pavlova

U KRÁLE JIŘÍHO

www.hotelkinggeorge.cz
Just off the Royal Way, this small hotel offers

COUNTRY COTTAGE

In days gone by many of the houses on the outskirts of the city were built of timber in log-cabin style. The only one remaining is U Raka (the "House at the sign of the Crayfish"), in the tranquil surroundings of Nový Svět in the Castle quarter. It has been turned into an exquisite and expensive little hotel, beautifully fitted out in rustic style, with just a few bedrooms. For more information visit www.romantikhotel-uraka.cz.
🚇 B6 ✉ Černínská 10, Hradčany ☎ 220 511 100 🚊 Tram 22, 23 to Brusnice

17 comfortable rooms. It also offers the dubious bonus of a music club on the ground floor.
🚇 F7 ✉ Liliová 10, Staré Město ☎ 261 264 309 🚊 Staroměstská

U KRÁLE KARLA

www.ukralekarla.cz
Nestling at the foot of the steps leading up to Hradčany Square, the comfortable King Charles exudes historic atmosphere, unsurprisingly, since the building it occupies goes back to the Middle Ages. Note that it's an uphill walk from the tram stop.
🚇 C7 ✉ Nerudova-Úvoz 4, Hradčany ☎ 257 531 211 🚊 Tram to Malostranské náměstí

U MEDVÍDKŮ

www.umedvidku.cz
The 43-room pension features beautiful beamed ceilings, decorated with Renaissance paintings. The famous pub of the same name is downstairs (▷ 42).
🚇 F8 ✉ Na Perštýně 7, Staré Město ☎ 224 211 916 🚊 Národní třída

UNION

www.hotelunion.cz
A 57-room art nouveau hotel with comfortable and stylish rooms set in a quiet square to the south of the city center.
🚇 G12 ✉ Ostrčilovo náměstí 4, Nusle ☎ 261 214 812 🚊 Tram 18, 24 to Ostrčilovo náměstí

Luxury Hotels

PRICES

Expect to pay upwards of 4,500Kč (over €160) per night for a luxury hotel.

ADRIA

www.adria.cz

Thoroughly modernized traditional hotel on Wenceslas Square. Rooms at the rear look out over the Franciscans' Garden.
➕ G8 ✉ Václavské náměstí 26 ☎ 221 081 111 Ⓜ Můstek

ARIA

www.ariahotel.net

An exquisite, very original 51-room hotel, designed and run on the theme of music. The rooftop terrace is lovely.
➕ D7 ✉ Tržiště 9, Malá Strana ☎ 225 334 111 🚋 Tram 12, 20, 22, 23 to Malostranské náměstí

BOSCOLO CARLO IV

www.boscolohotels.com

This magnificent neoclassical palace close to the main station and the Municipal House is now one of Prague's most sumptuous hotels.
➕ H7 ✉ Senovážné náměstí 13 ☎ 224 593 111 Ⓜ Hlavní nadráží or Náměstí Republiky

DŮM U TŘÍ ČÁPŮ

www.hotelthreestorks.cz

The "House at the Three Storks", a lovely little hotel dating from the 14th century, offers a wealth of design features.
➕ D6 ✉ Valdštejnská náměstí 8 ☎ 257 210 779 Ⓜ Malostranská

FOUR SEASONS HOTEL PRAGUE

www.fourseasons.com/prague

Luxurious conversion of a group of historic buildings near Charles Bridge. Its CottoCrudo restaurant (▷ 41) serves traditional Italian food with flair.
➕ F7 ✉ Veleslavínova 2a, Staré Město ☎ 221 427 000 Ⓜ Staroměstská

IRON GATE HOTEL & SUITES

www.irongate.cz

Luxury in a beautifully adapted 14th-century courtyard building in a cobbled street near Old Town Square.
➕ F7 ✉ Michalská 19, Old Town ☎ 225 777 777 Ⓜ Staroměstská or Můstek

JOSEF

www.hoteljosef.com

Design hotel featuring 109 rooms of cool luxury

OFFERS

The number of visitors to Prague has tended to stabilize, while provision of luxury accommodations has expanded rapidly. The rack rates charged by luxury hotels are as high as anywhere in the world, but most will offer substantial discounts at slack periods. It's well worth checking whether such offers are available while planning your trip.

with every conceivable amenity. Rooftop gym and sauna.
➕ G6 ✉ Rybná 20, Staré Město ☎ 221 700 111 Ⓜ Náměstí Republiky

K&K CENTRAL

www.kkhotels.com

The equal in terms of opulent art nouveau architecture to the famous Evropa, the Central easily outclasses its rival in its comfort, convenience and inventive adaptation.
➕ H7 ✉ Hybernská 10, Nové Město ☎ 225 022 000 Ⓜ Náměstí Republiky

MANDARIN ORIENTAL

www.mandarinoriental.com/Prague

This luxury hotel is a conversion of a 14th-century monastery in Malá Strana. The spa is in an adjoining building, with a whole range of tempting treatments.
➕ D7 ✉ Nebovidská 1, Malá Strana ☎ 233 088 888 🚋 Tram 12, 20, 22 to Hellichova

YASMIN

www.hotel-yasmin.cz

A significant addition to Prague's range of designer hotels, Yasmin upstages most of its rivals in sheer verve and trendiness. There's a Summer Garden and a Noodle Café and Bar.
➕ H7 ✉ Politických vězňů 12, Nove Město ☎ 234 100 100 Ⓜ Muzeum or Můstek

Need to Know

Use this section to help you plan your visit to Prague. We have suggested the best ways to get around the city and useful information for when you are there.

Planning Ahead

When to Go

The best times to visit are in spring, when the fruit trees of Petřín Hill are in blossom, and in early summer, before the throngs of tourists arrive. Most tourists visit between May and September. Christmas and New Year see the main squares become decorated markets and later rowdy New Year's Eve party sites.

> ### TIME
> Prague is one hour ahead of the UK, six hours ahead of New York and nine hours ahead of Los Angeles.

	AVERAGE DAILY MAXIMUM TEMPERATURES										
JAN	FEB	MAR	APR	MAY	JUN	JUL	AUG	SEP	OCT	NOV	DEC
30°F	32°F	39°F	48°F	57°F	63°F	66°F	64°F	57°F	48°F	39°F	32°F
-1°C	0°C	4°C	9°C	14°C	17°C	19°C	18°C	14°C	9°C	4°C	0°C

Spring (March–May) starts out cold and damp but turns beautiful in April and May, with blooming trees and gardens throughout the city.

Summer (June–August) can be oppressively hot and humid, with heavy rainfall.

Fall (September–November) is a lovely time, with bright, sunny days through October and dwindling numbers of tourists. The weather has cooled considerably by November.

Winter (December–February) can be depressingly gray and cold, with the occasional heavy snowfall to brighten the mood.

WHAT'S ON

May *Prague Spring Music Festival* (late March to early June): This international event (www.festival.cz) consists of an array of classical music concerts held in churches, palaces and halls throughout the city. It starts with a procession from Smetana's grave in the National Cemetery in Vyšehrad, where he was buried in 1884, to the great hall named after him in the restored Obecní dům (Municipal House), where a rousing performance of his orchestral tone poem

Má Vlast (My Country) is given.

June *Dance Prague*: International dance festival with events at various venues (www.tanecpraha.cz).

July/August Summer festivals of early music (www.tynska.cuni.cz).

Autumn *Agharta Prague Jazz Festival*: Going strong since 1992, this festival (www.agharta.cz) brings in jazz and blues acts from all over the world. It is sponsored by the Agharta jazz club (▷ 40) and is held in venues throughout the city.

December *St. Nicholas* (5 December): A multitude of St. Nicks roam the city's streets, accompanied by an angel who rewards good children with candy and a devil who chastizes appropriately.

Christmas Eve (24 December): Live carp are sold for the traditional Czech Christmas Eve dinner.

New Year's Eve (31 December): There are formal Sylvester balls and, outside, crowds welcome the arrival of the New Year on the streets.

Prague Online

www.prague-info.cz
Prague's leading hotel reservation site, with all categories of accommodation bookable online.

www.czechtourism.com
Czech Tourism's website provides information on agrotourism, UNESCO-graded monuments, cycling, mountaineering and other outdoor activities, along with practical planning advice.

www.praha.eu
Official web portal of the city of Prague. Overview of local events and a decent selection of tourist information and practical advice.

www.radio.cz
News, history, interesting features and details of upcoming events from Radio Prague.

www.expats.cz
A leading expat bulletin board with avertise-ments for jobs, as well as entertainment listings, tips on living in Prague and a variety of interesting articles.

www.praguemonitor.com
This online English-language "newspaper" is a good source of news on current events and cultural activities.

www.praguepost.com
The online version of the city's weekly English-language paper, with news, comprehensive listings, and some visitor information.

www.prague.tv
City guide with accommodations finder, restaurant and nightlife listings, expat gossip and survival tips.

www.motorway.cz/
This useful site (in English, too) on the Czech motorway network has maps, updated traffic news, driving advice and more.

USEFUL TRAVEL SITE

www.fodors.com
A complete travel-planning site. You can research prices and weather; make airline, car or room reservations; pose questions to fellow travelers; and find links to other sites.

INTERNET CAFÉS

Planeta
One of the city's best-value internet cafés.
🚩 H5 ✉ Ripská 24, Vinohrady ☎ 267 311 182; www.planeta.cz 🚇 Jiřího z Poděbrad 💷 From 0.26Kč per minute

The Globe
Coffee, food and books. Plug-ins for laptops.
🚩 E5 ✉ Pštrossova 6, Nové Město ☎ 224 934 203; www.globebookstore. cz 🚇 Národní třída 💷 1Kč per minute

Kava Kava Kava
Pleasant café serving good coffee. Free WiFi with a purchase. There are also computers downstairs for surfing.
🚩 D–E5 ✉ Národní 37 (in the Platýz courtyard), Staré Město ☎ 224 228 862; www.kava-coffee.cz 🚇 Národní třída 💷 60Kč per hour

Getting There

ENTRY REQUIREMENTS

Tourists from the UK, Canada, US and most European countries do not need visas. Be sure to check the latest entry requirements before visiting as they can change at short notice.

DRIVING

● Road regulations are much the same in the Czech Republic as in the rest of Europe. The alcohol limit for drivers is zero and spot checks are frequent.

● Speed limits in built-up areas (indicated by place-name signs) are 50kph (31mph). Outside built-up areas the limit is 90kph (56mph) and on motorways it is 130kph (80mph).

● A vignette (sticker) permitting the use of motorways must be purchased and displayed. Buy them at post offices or large petrol stations. Rental cars should already have them.

● Headlights must be on at all times.

● Trams must be given priority.

● First-aid kit, warning triangle and spare light bulbs must be carried.

AIRPORTS

Václav Havel Airport Prague is 10km (6 miles) northwest of the city center. It is served by direct flights from most major European cities, as well as New York and Atlanta. There are shops, bars and restaurants. The national airline is ČSA (head office: ✉ V Celnící 5, Nové Město ☎ 239 007 007).

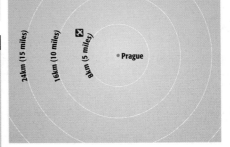

ARRIVING BY AIR

Airport information ☎ 220 113 314 (www. prg.aero). The most straightforward link from Václav Havel Airport to downtown is by minibus (Kč150 from the Cedaz desk in the arrivals hall) to CSA terminal, close to Náměstí Republiky on the eastern edge of the Old Town. Alternatively, the Airport Express (AE) bus (ticket Kč60 from driver) runs to the main rail station (Hlavní nádrazí) calling at Dejvice Metro station en route, from where it is only a few stops to downtown. Ordinary bus lines 100 and 119 (standard public transport ticket Kč36 from the DPP public transport office in the arrivals hall or from the ticket machine at the bus stop—coins required) connect to Zličín Metro (convenient for western parts of the city) and Dejvice Metro respectively. Night bus 510 follows a tortuous route to Karlovo náměstí, connecting with night tram 56 at Petřiny.

Taxis can be picked up at the airport, but agree on the approximate fare beforehand. The journey to the city center costs around Kč600–Kč700 and takes 25–45 minutes.

ARRIVING BY BUS

Express buses link Prague with international destinations, including London. The main coach terminal is at Florenc, on the eastern edge of downtown, where there is also a metro station. You can buy tickets at the coach terminal in Florenc but it is easier to use a travel agent.

ARRIVING BY CAR

Good main roads link Prague to all adjoining countries, and the city is now linked by motorway D5/E50 to the German autobahn network via Plzeň and the Bavarian border. The D8/E55 motorway toward Dresden and Berlin is almost complete. Prague is 1,100km (683 miles) from Calais (France), with its ferry services to Dover (UK) as well as the Channel Tunnel Shuttle. Public transportation in Prague is very good, so once in the city a car is likely to be more of a hindrance than a help.

ARRIVING BY TRAIN

Express trains connect Prague to all adjoining countries. The most convenient rail route from London is by Eurostar to Brussels, then German railways overnight trains via Frankfurt or Berlin. Most trains terminate at Hlavní nádraží (Main Station ✚ F4), though many stop (or terminate) at Holešovice in the northern suburbs or at Smíchov in the southern suburbs, both of which have good metro connections. Czech Railways (ČD) has information offices in Main Station at the north end of level 3 (domestic) and the south end of the lower hall (international) ☎ 840 112 113 (www.cd.cz).

INSURANCE

All visitors should have full medical and travel insurance even though the European Health Insurance Card (EHIC) entitles holders to free treatment. Taking out medical insurance ensures rapid repatriation and can help in cutting through bureaucracy.

DRIVING

● Delays due to road construction are frequent as the country builds up its highway infrastructure. Always budget a bit of extra time when driving.

● Check that your insurance policy covers you to drive in the Czech Republic.

● Aggressive driving is not uncommon. Resist the temptation to compete.

● No special license is needed for tourists who stay less than 90 days.

● The map *Praha pro motoristy* (Prague for Motorists) is an invaluable aid to driving in the city.

Getting Around

NATIONAL HOLIDAYS

1 January (St. Sylvester's Day), Easter Monday, 1 May (Labor Day), 8 May (Liberation Day), 5 July (SS Cyril and Methodius), 6 July (Jan Hus's Day), 28 September (St. Wenceslas's Day), 28 October (Independence Day), 17 November (Struggle for Freedom and Democracy Day), 24–26 December

TELEPHONES

● With the exception of emergency numbers, taxi dispatchers and the like, only 9-digit numbers are valid. If in doubt, call directory inquiries ☎ 1180.

● Most public phones now take phone cards, on sale in kiosks and post offices. Telephoning from your hotel may cost several times the standard rate.

● To call the Czech Republic from the UK, dial 00 420. To call the UK from Prague, dial 00 44, then drop the first zero from the area code.

● To call the Czech Republic from the US, dial 011 420. To call the US from Prague, dial 001.

PUBLIC TRANSPORT

● Public transport maps are available from the information offices at the airport and metro stations Muzeum, Anděl and Nádraží Holešovice.

● Expect crowding during the rush hours (generally 7am–10am, 3pm–6pm). The young and fit should give up their seats to passengers who need them more.

● Valid for all forms of transport, tickets cost Kč24 (short trips) or Kč32 (valid 1–1.5 hours) allowing as many changes as necessary. They must be validated in the machines provided before your journey. One- and three-day passes are available.

BUS

● Kept out of downtown to minimize pollution, buses serve all the suburban areas that the trams do not reach.

FUNICULAR

● The *lanovka* (funicular railway) climbs to the top of Petřín Hill from its Újezd station in Malá Strana via a halfway station at Nebozízek.

● You can use the normal Kč32 public transport ticket or the one- or three-day pass.

METRO

● This showpiece system, with its fast and frequent trains and clean stations, consists of three lines: A (coded green), B (yellow) and C (red). They converge from the suburbs onto downtown, where there are several interchange stations.

● To get on the right train, check the line (A, B or C) and note the name of the terminus station at the end of the line in the direction you wish to travel; this station appears on the overhead direction signs.

● Outlying stations are relatively far apart and are intended to feed commuters to connecting trams and buses.

● Particularly useful stations are Můstek (for Wenceslas Square and Old Town Square), Staroměstská (for Old Town Square) and Malostranská (for Malá Strana and for tram 22). Note that Hradčanská station is a good 15-minute walk from Prague Castle.

TAXIS
● Prague taxi drivers have a reputation for overcharging.
● Agree on the approximate fare beforehand and ask for a receipt: this should reduce excessive demands.
● You may receive a more reliable service if you phone for a taxi or flag down a moving taxi rather than going to a taxi rank in a tourist area, where drivers have the worst reputation.
● For taxis, telephone AAA Radiotaxi ☎ 222 333 222 or Profitaxi ☎ 261 314 151.
● Smart hotels have their own taxi service, reliable but expensive.

TRAMS
● The tramway system operates in close conjunction with the metro.
● The name of every tram stop appears on the stop sign and on the route map.
● Tram routes are numbered, and the tram has a destination board. Timetables are posted on the stop and are almost always adhered to.
● There is a skeleton service of night trams, with its own system of particular numbers and schedules from midnight until 4am.
● A particularly useful and scenic tram line is the No. 22, which runs from the city hub (at Národní třída) right through Malá Strana, past Malostranská metro station, then climbs to the back of Prague Castle (Pražský hrad stop) and continues to Strahov Monastery (Pohořelec stop).
● On weekends between April and November an old-timer tram (route No. 91) trundles along the tracks. It's a fun way of seeing the city.

MONEY
● There are plenty of cash machines in Prague, including at the airport, and instructions are usually given in English as well as Czech.

● Children, students and older people are entitled to discounts for many services and attractions in the city, though you might need to show your passport or student card to prove that you are eligible.

VISITORS WITH DISABILITIES
Many of the things that make Prague such an enchanting city—cobblestoned streets, red trams and Gothic towers with breathtaking views—can be notoriously difficult for visitors with disabilities to negotiate. The metro, too, has limited access; check which stations have facilities before traveling. The local organization Pražská organizace vozíčkářů (POV) produces a map-booklet to Prague for visitors with disabilities, which is available from tourist information centers. There is also information on accessible bus, metro and tram facilities at www.dpp.cz/en/barrier-free-travel/.

Essential Facts

BE UP-TO-DATE

Citizens of countries outside the EU should check visa regulations before traveling as these can change at short notice.

MONEY

The Czech crown (*koruna česká* or Kč) is divided into 100 virtually worthless hellers (*haléř*). There are coins for 1, 2, 5, 10, 20 and 50 crowns, and notes in denominations of 100, 200, 500, 1,000, 2,000 and 5,000 crowns.

CUSTOMS REGULATIONS

● Most non-commercial items imported into the Czech Republic for personal use are not subject to customs duty, though there are the usual limits on tobacco, alcohol and perfume. Similar conditions apply to the export of non-commercial items, though in the case of antiques and "rare cultural objects" it may be necessary to obtain an official certificate from a recognized museum or art gallery.

● Visitors from countries outside the EU can claim back the value-added tax on items purchased in the Czech Republic for more than Kč2,000. The receipt for such goods should be retained and presented to the customs official on leaving the country. See www.globalblue.com for details.

ELECTRICITY

● 220 volts, 50 cycles AC, fed through standard Continental two-pin round plugs.

ETIQUETTE

● Czech manners tend to be formal. Titles such as Doctor must not be ignored, and hands should be shaken when offered.

● Dress is less formal than it was. Neat casual wear is acceptable in most restaurants and tourist theaters. Smart dress is expected in other theaters and at the opera.

● Diners share tables in busy eateries and exchange greetings: *dobrý den* (good day) and *dobrou chut'* (enjoy your meal).

● Czechs invariably say *dobrý den* (hello) and *na shledanou* (goodbye) when entering or leaving an establishment.

● If you are invited to a Czech home, take flowers or a gift and remove your shoes at the door.

MONEY MATTERS

● There are bureaux de change, but banks and ATMs often give better exchange rates.

● Credit cards are in increasing use.

OPENING HOURS

● Banks: Mon–Fri 8/9–4/5.

● Shops: big malls and many downtown shops open until late weekdays, and at weekends; elsewhere hours are Mon–Fri 9–6, Sat 9–1.

● Museums and galleries: Tue–Sun 9/10–6 (opening times vary, especially for smaller sites). Most close Mon, except the National Museum and Prague Castle (open daily); the Jewish Museum is open Sun–Fri. Some museums also close for lunch.

PLACES OF WORSHIP

● Roman Catholic: sv Tomáše (St. Thomas's Church) 🖂 Josefská 8, Malá Strana 🚇 Malostranská 🕙 English Mass Sun 11am

● Anglican: sv Klimenta (St. Clement's Church) 🖂 Klimentská, Nové Město 🚇 Náměstí Republiky 🕙 Service Sun 11am (in English)

● Jewish: Staronová synagóga (Old/New Synagogue, ▷ 26–27) 🖂 Pařížská and Červená 🚇 Staroměstská 🕙 Services Fri sunset, Sat 9am

STUDENT VISITORS

● Few discounts are available for students.

● All aspects of youth travel are dealt with by the Student Agency 🖂 Revolučni 25, Nové Město 🕿 800 100 300 🚇 Náměstí Republiky

TOILETS

● WC, *muži/páni* (Men) and *ženy/dámy* (Women) are useful signs to remember.

● Public facilities are rare; look in restaurants, cafés, metro stations, etc.

● Public toilets often require a fee of Kč5/10.

The office is at 🖂 Karoliny Světlé 5, Staré Město 🕿 224 235 085

Visitors from EU countries, including Britain, are entitled to free emergency medical treatment, though a charge may be made for medicines. Make sure you have your blue European Health Insurance Card with you. Private medical insurance is necessary for citizens of other countries, and is still advised for EU citizens. Your hotel reception will help direct you to appropriate treatment facilities. Hospitals and clinics used to dealing with foreigners include:

Nemocnice Na Homolce
(public hospital)
✚ Off map A9
🖂 Roentgenova 2
🕿 257 271 111
🚌 167 from Anděl metro station to last stop

Canadian Medical Care
(private clinic)
✚ Off map A4
🖂 Veleslavínská 1
🕿 235 360 133
🚌 Tram 20, 26 to Nádraží Veleslavín

NEED TO KNOW **ESSENTIAL FACTS**

Language

Czech is a Slavonic (Slavic) language, particularly closely related to Slovak and Polish, less so to Russian and the South Slav languages. Like them it has a complex grammar and many inflections. Pronunciation can be a problem for foreigners, but one bonus is that the language, unlike English, is pronounced as it is written, invariably with the stress on the first syllable of the word. Most Czechs dealing with visitors from abroad will speak at least some English, but it is always worthwhile learning a few stock phrases and becoming familiar with signs.

SHOPPING

Can you assist me please? *Pomůžete mi, prosím?*

I'm looking for… *Hledám…*

Where can I buy…? *Kde dostanu…?*

How much is this/that? *Kolik stojí tohle/tamto?*

When does the shop open/close? *Kdy tady otevíráte/zavíráte?*

I'm just looking, thank you. *Děkují, jenom si prohlížím.*

I'll take this. *Vezmu si to.*

Do you have anything less expensive/ smaller/larger? *Máte něco levnějšího/menšího/většího?*

Are the instructions included? *Jsou u toho pokyny pro uživatele?*

Do you have a bag for this? *Máte na to tašku?*

I'd like a kilo of… *Prosím kilo…*

This is the right size. *To je správná velikost.*

Do you have this in…? *Máte to v…?*

Is there a market? *Je tady někde trh/tržnic?*

USEFUL WORDS

yes *ano*
no *ne*
please *prosím*
thank you *děkují*
you're welcome *prosím/nemáte zač*
excuse me! *Promiňte!*
where *kde*
here *tady*
there *tam*
when *kdy*
now *teď?*
later *později*
why *proč*
who *kdo*
may I/can I? *můžu?*

MONEY

Is there a bank/currency exchange office nearby?
Je tady někde blízko banka/směnárna?

I'd like to change sterling/dollars into crowns (Kč, Czech currency).
Anglické libry/americké dolary za české koruny (Kč) prosím.

Can I use my credit card to withdraw cash?
Mohu vybírat hotovost na svoji kreditní kartu?

GETTING AROUND

Where is the train/bus station?
Kde je tady železniční/autobusové nádraží?

Does this train/bus go to...?
Jede ten vlak/autobus do...?

Does this train/bus stop at...?
Staví ten vlak/autobus v...?

Please stop at the next stop.
Zastavte mi na další zastávce, prosím.

Where are we? *Kde jsme?*

Do I have to get off here? *Musím tady vystoupit?*

Where can I buy a ticket?
Kde si mohu koupit lístek?

Is this seat taken? *Je tady obsazeno?*

Where can I reserve a seat?
Kde si mohu rezervovat místo?

Please can I have a single/return ticket to...
Prosím jízdenku/zpáteční jízdenku do...

Where is the timetable? *Kde je jízdní řád?*

GENERAL QUERIES

Where is the tourist information office/desk, please? *Kde je informač středisko pro turisty, prosím?*

Do you have a city map?
Máte mapu města?

Can you give me some information about...?
Promiň informace o...?

What is the admission price?
Kolik stoji vstupné?

Are there guided tours? *Máte obhlídku s průvodcem?*

Can we make reservations here?
Můžeme si tady rezervovat?

How much is a ticket?
Kolík stojí lístek?

Where do they go?
Kam to jezdí?

DAYS OF THE WEEK

Monday *pondělí*
Tuesday *úterý*
Wednesday *středa*
Thursday *čtvrtek*
Friday *pátek*
Saturday *sobota*
Sunday *neděle*

Timeline

WHITE MOUNTAIN

In 1620 the Protestant army was routed at the Battle of White Mountain. Protestant leaders were executed in Old Town Square and Czechs who refused to reconvert to Catholicism emigrated en masse. A largely foreign nobility loyal to the Habsburgs, was installed, and Prague was beautified with churches and palaces. The court made Vienna its main seat and Prague became a sleepy provincial town.

FIRST REPUBLIC

Established in 1918, the First Czechoslovak Republic was a model democracy in many ways. However, it suffered from the insoluble problem of a large German minority.

From left: Václav Havel, first president of the Czech Republic; St. Vitus's Cathedral; the Soviet army occupy the city, 1968; Jan Palach memorial; John Lennon Wall; crosses representing executed noblemen; radical preacher Jan Hus

7th or 8th century *AD* Prague's legendary foundation by Princess Libuše.

10th century Trading settlements are set up in Lesser Town and Old Town.

1231 King Wenceslas I fortifies the Old Town with 13 towers, walls and a moat.

1253–78 Reign of King Otakar II, who extends and fortifies Lesser Town, inviting German merchants to settle there.

1415 Radical preacher Jan Hus is burned at the stake.

1576–1611 Reign of eccentric Emperor Rudolph II.

1620 Battle of White Mountain.

1848 Austrian General Windischgrätz puts down a revolt led by students, but Czech nationalism continues to grow.

1914–18 Czechs are dragged against their will into World War I on the Austrian side. Many soldiers desert or join the Czechoslovak Legion fighting for the Allies.

1938 Czechoslovakia is forced to give up the Sudetenland to Nazi Germany.

1939 Prague is occupied by Nazi Germany and not liberated until 1945.

1945–47 Expulsion of the 3 million German minority from Czechoslovakia.

1948 Communists in the government stage a coup d'état. Years of Stalinist repression follow.

1968 Prague Spring (▷ side panel).

1977 Dissident intellectuals sign Charter 77, a call for the government to apply the Helsinki Agreements of 1975. Many are harrassed and imprisoned.

1989 The Velvet Revolution. Václav Havel is chosen as president.

1993 Czechoslovakia splits into the independent states of Slovakia and Czech Republic.

1999 The Czech Republic joins NATO.

2002 Catastrophic floods wreak havoc in Prague and throughout the country.

2003 Havel is replaced as president by former prime minister, Eurosceptic Václav Klaus.

2004 The Czech Republic joins the European Union.

2011 On 18 December, former president Václav Havel dies.

2013 Prague is once again hit by flooding, leading to a mass evacuation of the city.

PRAGUE SPRING

In the Prague Spring of 1968, Czechoslovakia's Communist party, under Alexander Dubček, promised to create "Socialism with a human face". Terrified at this prospect, the Soviet Union sent tanks in and took members of the government off to Moscow in chains. The last Soviet troops did not leave until 1991.

PROTEKTORAT

In 1939, German troops marched into Prague, and Czechoslovakia became the "Protectorate" of Bohemia-Moravia. Nazi rule was brutal, spectacularly so after the assassination of Reichsprotektor Heydrich, while the Holocaust brought to an end 1,000 years of Jewish history in the Czech lands. In May 1945, after the longest Nazi occupation in any European country, the people of Prague liberated their city and welcomed in the Red Army.

Index

INDEX

127

Published by AA Publishing, a trading name of AA Media Limited, whose registered office is Fanum House, Basing View, Basingstoke, Hampshire RG21 4EA. Registered number 06112600.

© **AA Media Limited 2016**
First published 1996
New edition 2016

WRITTEN BY Michael Ivory
UPDATED BY Mark Baker
SERIES EDITOR Clare Ashton
DESIGN WORK Tracey Freestone
INDEXER Marie Lorimer
IMAGE RETOUCHING AND REPRO Ian Little

Colour separation by AA Digital Department
Printed and bound by Leo Paper Products, China

A CIP catalogue record for this book is available from the British Library.

ISBN 978-0-7495-7804-6

A05378
Maps in this title produced from mapping © MAIRDUMONT / Falk Verlag 2012
Transport map © Communicarta Ltd, UK

The Automobile Association would like to thank the following photographers, companies and picture libraries for their assistance in the preparation of this book.

2/3t AA/C Sawyer; 4/18t AA/S McBride; 4 AA/J Wyand; 5 AA/S McBride; 6cl AA/C Sawyer; 6cc AA/J Wyand; 6cr AA/S McBride; 6bl AA/C Sawyer; 6bc AA/J Smith; 6br AA/S McBride; 7cl AA/T Souter; 7ccl AA/J Smith; 7ccr AA/S McBride; 7cr AA/C Sawyer; 7bl AA/C Sawyer; 7bcl AA/C Sawyer; 7bcr AA/J Smith; 7br AA/S McBride; 8/9t AA/S McBride; 10tr AA/J Smith; 10ctr AA/J Smith; 10/11c AA/J Wyand; 10/1b AA/C Sawyer; 11tl AA/S McBride; 11cl AA/J Smith; 13tl Digitalvision; 13ctl AA/J Smith; 13c AA/J Wyand; 13cbl AA/J Wyand; 13bl AA/J Wyand; 14tr AA/J Smith; 14tcr AA/J Wyand; 14bcr AA/J Smith; 14br AA/J Smith; 16t AA/J Smith; 16tc AA/J Smith; 16bc AA/S McBride; 16b AA/J Smith; 17t AA/J Smith; 17tc AA/J Wyand; 17bc Image 100; 17b AA/J Smith; 18tc AA/J Wyand; 18c AA/C Sawyer; 18cb AA/S McBride; 18b AA/C Sawyer; 19(I) AA/J Wyand; 19(II) AA/J Smith; 19(III) AA/J Wyand; 19(IV) AA/J Smith; 19(V) AA/C Sawyer; 20/1 AA/S McBride; 24l AA/J Smith; 24/5 AA/J Smith; 25r AA/J Smith; 26l AA/J Smith; 26tr AA/J Smith; 26br AA/J Smith; 26/7b AA/J Smith; 27tl AA/J Smith; 27bl AA/J Smith; 27r AA/J Smith; 28l AA/J Smith; 28/9t AA/S McBride; 28/9b AA/S McBride; 29t AA/J Smith; 29bl AA/S McBride; 29br AA/S McBride; 30l AA/S McBride; 30c AA/S McBride; 30r AA/S McBride; 31 AA/J Smith; 32l AA/J Smith; 32/3tr AA/J Wyand; 32br AA/C Sawyer; 33t AA/C Sawyer; 33bl AA/S McBride; 33br AA/J Smith; 34l AA/J Smith; 34c AA/J Smith; 34r AA/J Smith; 35t AA/J Wyand; 35bl AA/J Smith; 35r AA/J Smith; 35/36t AA/J Wyand; 36bl AA/S McBride; 37 AA/J Smith; 38 AA/J Smith; 39 AA/J Smith; 40t AA/J Wyand; 41 AA/J Smith; 42t AA/S McBride; 43 AA/J Wyand; 46l AA/J Smith; 46r AA/S McBride; 47l AA/C Sawyer; 47r AA/J Smith; 48l AA/J Wyand; 48r AA/J Wyand; 49l AA/S McBride; 49r AA/J Smith; 50/1t AA/S McBride; 50bl AA/J Smith; 50br AA/J Wyand; 51tl AA/J Smith; 50/1bl AA/J Smith; 51c AA/S McBride; 51r AA/C Sawyer; 52 AA/J Smith; 52/3t AA/J Smith; 52/3b AA/J Smith; 53 AA/J Smith; 54t AA/J Wyand; 54bl AA/J Smith; 54br AA/J Wyand; 55t AA/J Wyand; 55bl AA/J Wyand; 55br AA/J Smith; 56 AA/J Smith; 57 AA/J Smith; 58 Photodisc; 59 Photodisc; 60t Digitalvision; 61 AA/J Smith; 62 AA/T Harris; 63 AA/J Smith; 66 AA/J Wyand; 67l AA/C Sawyer; 67r AA/J Wyand; 68 AA/J Wyand; 68/9t AA/J Wyand; 68br AA/J Wyand; 69t AA/C Sawyer; 68/9b AA/S McBride; 69br AA/C Sawyer; 70l AA/S McBride; 70c AA/S McBride; 70r AA/S McBride; 71l AA/J Smith; 71r AA/J Smith; 72 AA/J Smith; 72/3t AA/C Sawyer; 72/3b AA/S McBride; 73t AA/S McBride; 73bl AA/S McBride; 73br AA/S McBride; 74l AA/J Wyand; 74/5 AA/S McBride; 75 AA/S McBride; 76t AA/J Wyand; 76bl AA/J Smith; 76br AA/C Sawyer; 77t AA/J Wyand; 77bl AA/T Souter; 77br AA/J Smith; 78 AA/J Smith; 79t AA/J Smith; 79b AA/J Smith; 80 AA/T Souter; 81 AA/T Souter; 84 AA/S McBride; 84/5 AA/S McBride; 85t AA/S McBride; 85bl AA/S McBride; 85br AA/S McBride; 86l AA/J Smith; 86c AA/J Smith; 86r AA/S McBride; 87l AA/J Smith; 87r AA/J Wyand; 88l AA/C Sawyer; 88r AA/J Wyand; 89/90t AA/J Wyand; 89b AA/J Wyand; 90bl AA/C Sawyer; 90br AA/C Sawyer; 91 AA/J Smith; 92t Photodisc; 92c Brand X Pics; 93/94t AA/C Sawyer; 95 AA/C Sawyer; 98 AA/J Wyand; 98/9t AA/J Wyand; 98/9b AA/C Sawyer; 99t AA/J Wyand; 99bl AA/C Sawyer; 99br AA/C Sawyer; 100t AA/J Smith; 100bl AA/J Smith; 100br AA/J Smith; 100/1t AA/J Smith; 101bl AA/J Smith; 101br AA/J Smith; 102l AA/J Wyand; 102r AA/J Smith; 103t AA/J Wyand; 103l AA/J Smith; 103r AA/J Wyand; 104t AA/J Wyand; 104bl AA/C Sawyer; 104br AA/C Sawyer; 105t AA/J Wyand; 105bl AA/C Sawyer; 105bcl AA/C Sawyer; 105bcr AA/J Wyand; 105br AA/J Wyand; 106t AA/J Wyand; 106bl AA/J Wyand; 106br AA/J Wyand; 107 AA/J Smith; 108t AA/C Sawyer; 108tr AA/J Smith; 108tcr AA/J Smith; 108c AA/S McBride; 108br AA/J Smith; 109/112t AA/C Sawyer; 113 AA/J Smith; 114/125 AA/J Wyand; 117 AA/J Smith; 121 AA/C Sawyer; 122c AA/J Wyand; 124bl AFP/Getty Images; 124cbl The AA; 124cbr Popperfoto/Getty Images; 124br AA/J Wyand; 125bl AA/J Wyand; 125bc AA/C Sawyer; 125br The AA

Every effort has been made to trace the copyright holders, and we apologise in advance for any accidental errors. We would be happy to apply the corrections in the following edition of this publication.

Titles in the Series